Idaho's Historic Trails

From Lewis & Clark to Railroads

Idaho's Historic Trails

From Lewis & Clark to Railroads

Martin Potucek

Caxton Press
Caldwell, Idaho
2003

ISBN 0-87004-432-x

Library of Congress Cataloging-in-Publication Data

Potucek, Martin, 1950-
Idaho's historic trails : from Lewis and Clark to railroads / by Martin Potucek.
p. cm.
Includes bibliographical references.
ISBN 0-87004-432-X
1. Historic sites--Idaho. 2. Trails--Idaho--History. 3. Roads--Idaho--History. 4. Idaho--History, Local. 5. Idaho--Description and travel. 6. Idaho--Tours. 7. Historic sites--Idaho--Guidebooks. 8. Trails--Idaho--Guidebooks. 9. Roads--Idaho--Guidebooks. 10. Automobile travel--Idaho--Guidebooks. I. Title.
F747 .P68 2003
979.6--dc21 2002153512

Lithographed and bound in the United States of America
Caxton Press
Caldwell, Idaho
169304

Contents

Maps viii
Illustrations ix
Acknowledgments xi
Introduction xv

1 Lewis and Clark 1
2 David Thompson and Kullyspell House 25
3 The Oregon Trail 37
4 George Wright and the United Tribes 59
5 Bear River Massacre 79
6 The Magruder Corridor .93
7 Nez Perce War 109
8 Warren Wagon Road 137
9 Railroads Through the Bitterroots 153

The Author 164
Bibliography 165

MAPS

Lewis and Clark through Idaho xx
Lewis & Clark Trail — Lolo Motorway 8
North Idaho Panhandle 24
Kullyspell House region 32
Oregon Trail in Idaho 38-39
Wright Expedition route 64-65
Preston area 78
Battle of Bear River 84
Magruder Corridor 92
Nez Perce homeland 108
Nez Perce War — Clearwater region 120
Nez Perce War — sites of interest .124
Warren Wagon Road 136
Rails over the Bitterroots 152

Illustrations

Rock Cairn at Indian Post Office, Lolo Trail 6
Trapper Peak from the Bitterroot Valley 11
Lolo Hot Springs today 13
New visitor center at Lolo Pass 15
Rocky Ridge Lake looking north from FR 500 16
Looking south over Wendover Ridge 17
Lochsa River at Powell, Idaho 19
Where Lewis and Clark made contact with the Nez Perces 21
Kootenai River looking west toward Bonners Ferry 27
Kullyspell House site 29
Kootenai River trail 30
Kootenai River at start of FR 24 35
Soda Point/Sheep Rock near Soda Springs 42
Lava Hot Springs on the Oregon Trail motor route 45
Register Rock at Massacre Rocks State Park 46
Conestoga wagon, Three Island Crossing State Park 48
Three Island Crossing Visitor Center, Glenns Ferry 49
Wagon ruts in sandstone on Sinker Butte 51
Sinker Creek Grade, Oregon Trail South Alternate 52
Ward Massacre site, south of Middleton, Idaho 53
Boise River crossing at Canyon Hill 54
Old Fort Boise site 57
Fort Boise in its heyday 57
The Cataldo Mission is Idaho's oldest building 63
Cataldo Mission interior 66
Hanging Camp site on Hangman Creek 71
Vandalized marker at Hanging Camp 72
Monument with Bear River Massacre site in background 83
Historical signboards and monument at massacre site 85
Plaque honors Morman women 86
Franklin, Idaho 89
Hill Beachy 94
Western end of Magruder Corridor (FR 468) 95
Looking south toward Salmon River from Nez Perce Pass 97
Red River Hot Springs 99
Sign marks the route to the Magruder murder site 100
View from Dry Saddle, looking west 103
Deep Creek Bridge 105
Westbound on Magruder Corridor. 106
Tolo Lake, a Nez Perce gathering place near Grangeville 113

Hayfield on John Day Creek where Henry Elfers was killed. . . 115
French Cemetery near Salmon River and White Bird 116
White Bird battlefield today, looking upslope 118
Swartz Pond at White Bird battlefield 119
Rocks where Rains command was wiped out 123
Clearwater battlefield 125
Musselshell Meadow 128
Mammoth replica at Grangeville, Idaho 130
Weis Rockshelter near Cottonwood 133
North Beach, North Fork Payette River 139
Forest Highway 21 near the north end of Payette Lake 140
Secesh Summit looking west 141
Warren Dance Hall 145
East end of Warren viewed from old schoolyard 146
Warren Guard Station at east end of town 149
West Portal of the Taft Tunnel, Hiawatha Rail Trail 154
Trail head near East Portal of Taft Tunnel 157
Rail Trail trestle 160

The Author 164

Acknowledgments

Of those who helped with this book, Merle Wells would have to be the first and most important influence. I met Merle in the last few years of his life, still spry and adventurous enough to pedal around Boise on his raspberry-colored bike. We met when I pestered him about his own life and an article I was preparing for a local press. The article, it turns out (a favorite phrase of his), ended up being the least of what I got from him that first interview. More than a sketch of his story, I walked away with a sense of living history, not two-dimensional from a book, but stories of people struggling to shape the land, or struggling just to remain on it. Stories unfolded of cultures from afar mixing with—and at times—shattering the local cultures.

Merle cared deeply that the historical records were accurate, that they were beyond political or moral agendas. His commitment to making the local histories accessible to the public has no better evidence than the historical signboards for which he researched and wrote the text. Those markers, over 200 in number, identify locations of historical significance across the entire state of Idaho. For over forty years, he was steward, guide, and archivist for the state's historical records.

Idaho State Historian Larry Jones in Boise was also essential to the writing of this book. Never too busy when I imposed myself, unannounced, to ask for clarification on this or that, Larry was gracious with his time and knowledge. The Idaho State Historical Society and Archives people were also helpful in answering my odd requests and questions. The Idaho State Library and its hard-working staff were also excellent in allowing me access to whatever I needed; sometimes it was the name of an obscure website, a reference work, or just a quiet place to study.

Dan Misciagna of the Idaho Panhandle National Forest in Bonners Ferry was helpful with directions to trails along the Kootenai River for the David Thompson chapter. Mark Wendle at Samowen was kind enough to show me the probable site of Kullyspell House, which is now not easily accessible. Clint Watkins out of Spokane, who has tramped over a good portion of David Thompson's Lake Indian Trail, helped to identitify and clarify portions of that route, as did Tom Sandberg, archaeologist for IPNF, out of Sandpoint.

Phil Cernera, biologist with the Coeur d'Alene Tribe, gave me some great information on the Trail of the Coeur d'Alenes. Leo Hennessy of Idaho State Parks and Recreation was also quite helpful in giving me background information on the history and process of that amazing cooperative achievement. Fred Bear and the folks at Heyburn State Park were candid and helpful. Heyburn is one of those special places in Idaho; capable stewardship there has preserved much of the natural beauty while allowing public access.

Larry Kingsbury, archaeologist and historian with the Payette National Forest in McCall, deserves thanks for his gracious and open manner. He and his staff went out of their way to show me their work in Warren, one of Idaho's great gold rush towns. Larry's work to execute the intent of the Cultural Heritage Program is excellent. It's programs like this that will ensure that the history, perhaps even parts of the pre-history, of the region will be preserved.

Sandi McFarland, Nez Perce National Trail Coordinator from the Clearwater country, presented me with some timely information on the Lolo Trail. Her energy and enthusiasm show a genuine respect for the trail and its significance. Robin Johnston, archaeologist at Clearwater National Forest in Kamiah, took the time to show me the route the Nee Mee Poo followed as they fled the Battle of the Clearwater. His explanations of the cultural differences between the fleeing Nez Perce and the pursuing army went a long way to broaden my understanding of the aftermath of the Battle of the Clearwater.

Thanks also to Theresa at the Slate Creek Forest Service office (Nez Perce National Forest) for her great energy and interest in the local history. Norman Blewett of Kooskia deserves special thanks for taking the time and effort to guide me to the Clearwater Battle site, where he noted he had ancestors on both sides of that encounter.

In researching the Rails over the Bitterroots chapter, Cort Sims' archaeological work for the Idaho Panhandle National Forest out of Coeur d'Alene laid the foundation for the wonderful signboards that grace the Route of the Hiawatha rail trail. It was Jamie Scmidt who wrote the text, and Grady Myers who produced the high level graphical depictions for those signs. Dennis Baird at the University of Idaho Library in Moscow also consulted on the history of the rail trail.

Introduction

The purpose of this book is to provide a mechanism for the general public to explore Idaho's history. "Explore" is used here in two senses: one—to explore in the everyday and mundane sense, learning by books and secondary sources, and two—to explore physically and directly, by roaming the earth and seeing for oneself. That's why this book is not just for reading; it's meant to be used as a reference tool for readers to find their way in the physical world and learn about the exploits described within. That may seem a subtle distinction for someone who reads and travels a lot, but finding yourself at a place like Weis Rock Shelter, where ancestors of the Nez Perce lived continuously for 8,000 years, petrifies context for the 1877 struggle between that tribe and the United States government.

The book should be of great value to people who get out and actually travel the routes described in these nine chapters. Every region of Idaho's vast and varied landscape is represented here. Our journey takes us to the austere surroundings of the Bear River in southeastern Idaho where the largest single annihilation of Native Americans by Europeans in this nation's history took place. We also go to the shores of Lake Pend Oreille in the far north of the state where an intrepid Englishman set up the first outpost in the Northwest to trade with natives.

Territory isn't the only thing spanned in this guide. Time, too, is traversed. The guide spans more than 150 years of exploration and struggle, from the passage of Lewis and Clark's Corps of Discovery through Idaho in

1805-1806 to the construction of a railroad across the same region more than a century later. Idaho represented one of the last unexplored regions of a rising power in a new age.

Although even today Idaho is an unknown to residents of many other states, particularly those in the Eastern U.S., the region is rich in western expansion history. For instance: most stories about the Oregon Trail, both in books and in the movies, focus on incidents that occurred on the Great Plains—Nebraska and Wyoming. But Idaho contains one of the most torturous and dangerous sections of the fabled route. The trail was rougher and the rivers that had to be crossed were deeper and swifter than farther east. More emigrants were killed by native attacks in Idaho than in any other state.

Idaho's destiny as a late-blooming child seems to be fulfilling itself even up to the moment of this writing. Since the 1960s the state has been a Mecca for people seeking refuge from the rat race of modern life. Perhaps what is more significant is Idaho's continued attraction as a place for recreation and revival. Cities such as Boise and Coeur d' Alene are among the fastest growing in the country. But they have somehow managed to maintain their charm and quality of life.

The beauty and diversity of Idaho's distinct regions defy verbal description. That is part of the aim of this book—to introduce newcomers and locals alike to some of the backwaters and obscure places with historical significance. Sometimes these places are far up in the mountains, and sometimes they're right next to a freeway where thousands of vehicles pass every day.

Much of the region's history lies hidden, but a little knowledge can help you find the keys to local history. Scholars have toiled for the past century to record this information, but in the past two decades a new movement has taken root. Tribal-private-public projects like the Trail of the Coeur d' Alenes have resurrected old railroad right-of-ways as public pathways. Non-profits like the Taft Tunnel Preservation Society are collaborating with national forest managers to create projects like the Route of the Hiawatha across the crest of the Bitterroot Mountains. In both of these recent examples, historical signage, kiosks, literature and websites are designed to make these places more accessible to the public in a physical and historical sense. We are fortunate to have so many people in the state willing to work together to preserve and support these trails.

Many people have stories about teachers who inspired them when they were younger. I didn't meet my teacher for this lesson until I was in my late forties. Merle Wells, Idaho's state historian and keeper of the state historical records for more than forty years, was my inspirational teacher. We met when he was close to eighty; until his death he was still pursuing what he most loved: untangling the history of the region known as Idaho. It was Merle who researched and wrote texts for the state historical signboards. Those signs were my first experience with his work, as I stopped to read them when first traversing the state.

The nine events covered by this volume are well known; they are some of the pivots on which the region's history has turned. If you want more detailed accounts of these stories they are better told by the experts, the scholars like Merle, who spent much of their lives separating reality from fabrication and myth. My aim is to tell the basic story and to give the reader the means to follow the actual path the event followed. This guidebook is meant to lead readers of events past through the reality of our modern world. Sometimes the traces of these events are still visible, but often all evidence has been obliterated except for the markers, monuments and parks erected to commemorate them.

This book is another form of marker that bids you to more than remember; it invites you to explore the early pathways. Whether you are cruising the interstate at seventy-five miles-an-hour, rolling along a dusty single track, paddling a Class 3 rapid, or just wandering through an ancient meadow, consider this: someone went this way before you. We can never know all the stories of those who have gone before, but of the ones where a record remains, we can learn which way we came. Perhaps, by knowing our previous pathways, including blunders and wrong turns, we may know which way to proceed.

Martin Potucek
June, 2003

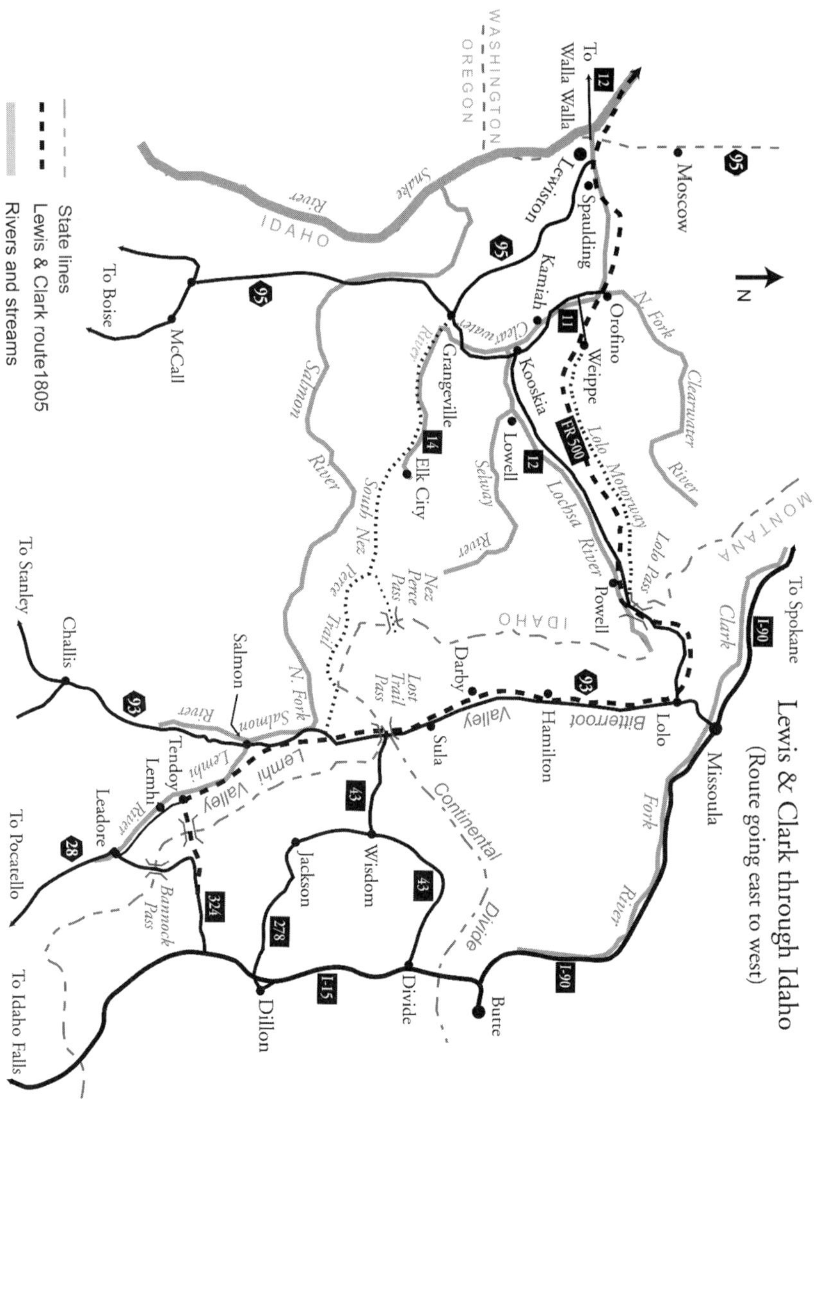
Lewis & Clark through Idaho
(Route going east to west)
State lines
Lewis & Clark route1805
Rivers and streams
WASHINGTON
OREGON
IDAHO
MONTANA
To Walla Walla
To Spokane
To Boise
To Stanley
To Pocatello
To Idaho Falls
Moscow
Lewiston
Spaulding
Kamiah
Orofino
Weippe
Kooskia
Lowell
Grangeville
Elk City
Powell
Lolo Pass
Lolo Motorway
Lolo
Missoula
Darby
Hamilton
Sula
Lost Trail Pass
Nez Perce Pass
South Nez Perce Trail
Salmon
Challis
Tendoy
Lemhi
Leadore
Bannock Pass
Lemhi Valley
Wisdom
Jackson
Divide
Dillon
Butte
McCall
Bitterroot Valley
Continental Divide
Snake River
Clearwater River
N. Fork Clearwater River
Lochsa River
Selway River
Salmon River
N. Fork Salmon River
Lemhi River
Clark Fork River
FR 500
12
95
11
14
93
43
28
324
278
I-90
I-15
N

Chapter One

Lewis and Clark in Idaho

Lewis and Clark first entered what is now Idaho on August 12, 1805, over Lemhi Pass. They had spent more than a year crossing the Mississippi River Valley and the Great Plains by following the Missouri River upstream. They were now at the threshold of the last great obstacle: the Rocky Mountains. Lewis had gone on ahead with a small party to scout the route while Clark remained with the main group at Camp Fortunate to cache the canoes and some supplies for the return trip. On foot now, they would have to find horses. *Significance: By going west over the mountains from the Beaverhead River, instead of north through the Big Hole, it would take them precious extra weeks, eventually crossing the Bitterroot Range three times on their way west.*

Not only is Lemhi Pass the border between Idaho and Montana, it also is the Continental Divide. Rather than joy after reaching this momentous spot, Lewis experienced dread because, from this vantage point, he could see the towering ranges of the Lemhi Range and the Salmon River mountains. He knew then that it would not be all downhill to the Pacific from here. Rather, these huge obstacles would have to be crossed or circumvented. His primary directive from Jefferson had been to find a water route to the Pacific, a commercial link to span the continent. Lewis, at this point, probably knew that was not to be.

By the time the expedition reached this point it had been gone fifteen months and traveled more than 3,000 miles west from Camp Wood, Illinois where it started on May 14, 1804. This was also the highest point the explorers would cross in their entire expedition (7,373 ft.). From here, Lewis could look down into the Lemhi Valley, which runs north-south; this would be a pivotal point in the adventure. The significance of this place was to go beyond route-finding and figuring out the geography. This was the peak of summer and it looked like the highest mountains were yet ahead of them. September, they knew, would bring snow to those peaks.

Guessing correctly that they had traversed the Great Divide, how could there be towering, snow-capped peaks rising to the west above them? Lewis had hoped that once across the divide, it would be an easy trip downstream to the Pacific Ocean. But only fifteen miles west was a range of peaks rising to nearly 11,000 feet.

On August 13, Lewis's small party moved down into the valley. There they came upon the Lemhi band of the Shoshoni native people, headed by Chief Cameahwait. This was an especially important point for the explorers because they needed to find horses to travel west across the mountains. It took Clark some effort to convince Cameahwaite to venture east over the pass to help Clark and the main party. The chief's reluctance was well-founded; for generations, the better armed Plains tribes (especially the Blackfeet) raided the Shoshoni summer camps, taking lives and slaves. The Lemhi Shoshonis stayed high and north of their Snake River brothers. They followed the buffalo on the eastern slope only late in the season when they could gather in sufficient numbers to defend themselves.

Lewis succeeded in persuading Cameahwaite and a group of warriors to backtrack and reunite with Clark's group back at the Red Rock River in western Montana. This was Camp Fortunate, now under the waters of Clark Canyon Reservoir. This was also the place where the chief, through unlikely coincidence, was reunited with his lost sister, Sacajewea. She had been kidnapped years before by Indian raiders (Minitaris), and amazingly, had been brought a thousand miles east, married a French trader named Charbonneau, who was then hired by the expedition as translator and guide. Now her circle was complete, for this group of white explorers, searching for a route through to the Pacific, had delivered her back to her home.

While Lewis's advance party had been gone, Clark cached canoes and provisions for their return trip; this would lighten their load going west over the mountains, but days were getting shorter, and nights colder. The reunited corps and brother and sister returned west over the divide and down to the village of Sacajewea's people. She helped to translate at a council between her brother, Cameahwait, and the captains. They were able to trade for twenty-nine horses, not enough for every man in the Corps of Discovery, but enough to speed them on their way .

Cameahwaite invited the expedition to winter with them here, and advised them not to attempt crossing the mountains so late in the season. But when Lewis heard that a large tribe lived just to the west of the mountains, and traveled across and back every year, he was determined to go. They would meet this friendly tribe and head for the sea. After a few days rest, diplomacy, and celebration at the chief's camp (near present Tendoy) the party headed north, taking on a guide nicknamed Old Toby and his son. The expedition made good time as it headed up Lemhi, and then the Salmon River valleys.

At North Fork, about fifteen miles north of Salmon, Clark took some men and explored west down the main Salmon River. Both Lewis and Clark knew that if they could find a water route through the mountains, it would be much faster than climbing over the mountains. Toby warned him away, but Clark made a strenuous detour down into the gorge. Clark's foray took him and a small band five days in and out of the rock-walled, whitewater canyon just to verify that. They made it as far as Indian Creek, about ten miles west of North Fork He reported the Salmon as utterly impassable; it was later to be called "The River of No Return."

At a place north of North Fork, where Hughes Creek spills down into the upper Salmon Valley, the ancient South Nez Perce Trail wound west up through the main spine of the Bitterroot Range. There's speculation about whether Toby consulted with Clark about it. This more southern route was shorter but higher, and involved a more torturous crossing of the mountains.

Toby took over as guide of the party as they approached what would later be called Lost Trail Pass. On September 2, 1805, they slowed to a crawl as Toby missed the lower pass and took them a thousand feet higher than they needed to go. Even building a trail as they went over some very rocky terrain didn't prevent them from losing three horses. This crossing was not an established native route; the expedition was breaking trail over some very steep and rocky terrain here. They would avoid this on their return trip and go back through Wisdom, Montana.

Once over the pass, they descended into the Bitterroot Valley of Montana. There, near Sula, they met a band of Flatheads (Salish), where they were able to trade for more rested horses and three colts. This was known as Ross Hole, after Alexander Ross. The colts would be emergency food, if needed, in crossing the mountains. Making good time again, they passed through present day Hamilton to arrive at the site of what later became the town of Lolo. Camping there September 9 and 10, where Lolo Creek dumps into the Bitterroot River, they named it Traveler's Rest.

After the two days' rest the expedition headed up the Lolo Trail, which was an ancient track used by the Nez Perce and others. The trail was steep and narrow, but it allowed the tribes west of the Bitterroots to access the buffalo country of the western Plains. Unfortunately, the explorers met with rainy and cold weather during the ascent, and this slowed their progress greatly. Staying mostly to the north side of Lolo Creek, they picked their way. One pleasant surprise on their approach to the pass was Lolo Hot Springs, An unpleasant surprise was the maze of trails that traversed the area; this truly was a pivotal point for native paths.

The party crossed over Lolo Pass about a mile south of the highway, proceeded down another couple miles of gentle slope to camp in Packer Meadows. Toby became confused, however, and led the party down the Lochsa River drainage rather than sticking to the ridge just north, where the main trail was located. On September 14, they reached the site of the present Powell Ranger Station. Exhausted and nearly out of food and supplies, with game scarce, the men had to kill a young colt to eat that night; They named the creek there Colt Killed Creek, now White Sand Creek

Martin Potucek photo

Rock Cairn at Indian Post Office, near the summit of the Lolo Trail.

On September 15, they went about four miles downstream on the Lochsa, and discovering their mistake, decided to hike up the steep ridge (Wendover Ridge) to the north. The difficult ascent resulted in falls by both horses and men. Once on top of the ridge, they regained the Indian trail, but they were dismayed at the sight of the seemingly endless mountains.

On September 16, they awoke to four inches of snow, and it continued snowing all day. They proceeded the next day through a high meadow with rock cairns known as the Indian Post Office, in knee-deep snow. This was the high point in crossing these mountains: elevation 7,033 ft. It would be another four days (ten days in all to cross the Bitterroots) before they would drag themselves, starving and weakened, out of the mountains, and onto Weippe Prairie.

On September 18, Captain Clark with a small group went to hunt and scout ahead. Clark's advanced party first spied the prairies to the west on this day from what's now called Sherman Peak. On the 19th, Clark came upon a stray horse they killed, and after taking breakfast from it, hung it up for Lewis and the main party as they followed. This was the closest the expedition would come on the entire trip to starving. They were desperate for food.

On September 20, Clark's small band broke out of the woods and onto a wide grassy plain. This was the Weippe Prairie, ancestral gathering place of the tribe the Shoshonis had told them about. Coming upon three Nez Perce youths in an open meadow, they finally made contact. After the youngsters were reassurred that the strangers meant no harm, they ran off with presents to tell their elders of these strange white men. Welcomed into the Indian camp, the hungry scouts were given dried buffalo, camas root, and berries.

Lewis and the main body of the expedition were about twenty miles behind, moving slower in a larger group, and starving. They luckily found the remains of the horse Clark had slaughtered and left for them. Lewis's men added a wolf and some pheasants they had shot that day. On September 22, Lewis's group stumbled out into the prairie where it was warmer, drier, and there was abundant grass for the horses.

Later that day Clark's and Lewis's groups reunited at a Nez Perce village above Lolo Creek (the Idaho Lolo Creek) just west of present day Weippe. Dried salmon, berries, and camas roots were obtained from the natives and the men were in high spirits, despite a serious stomach flu that seems to have attacked all of the expedition (some suspect the camas roots were to blame). Twisted Hair was the closest chief in the area not off hunting, and so the

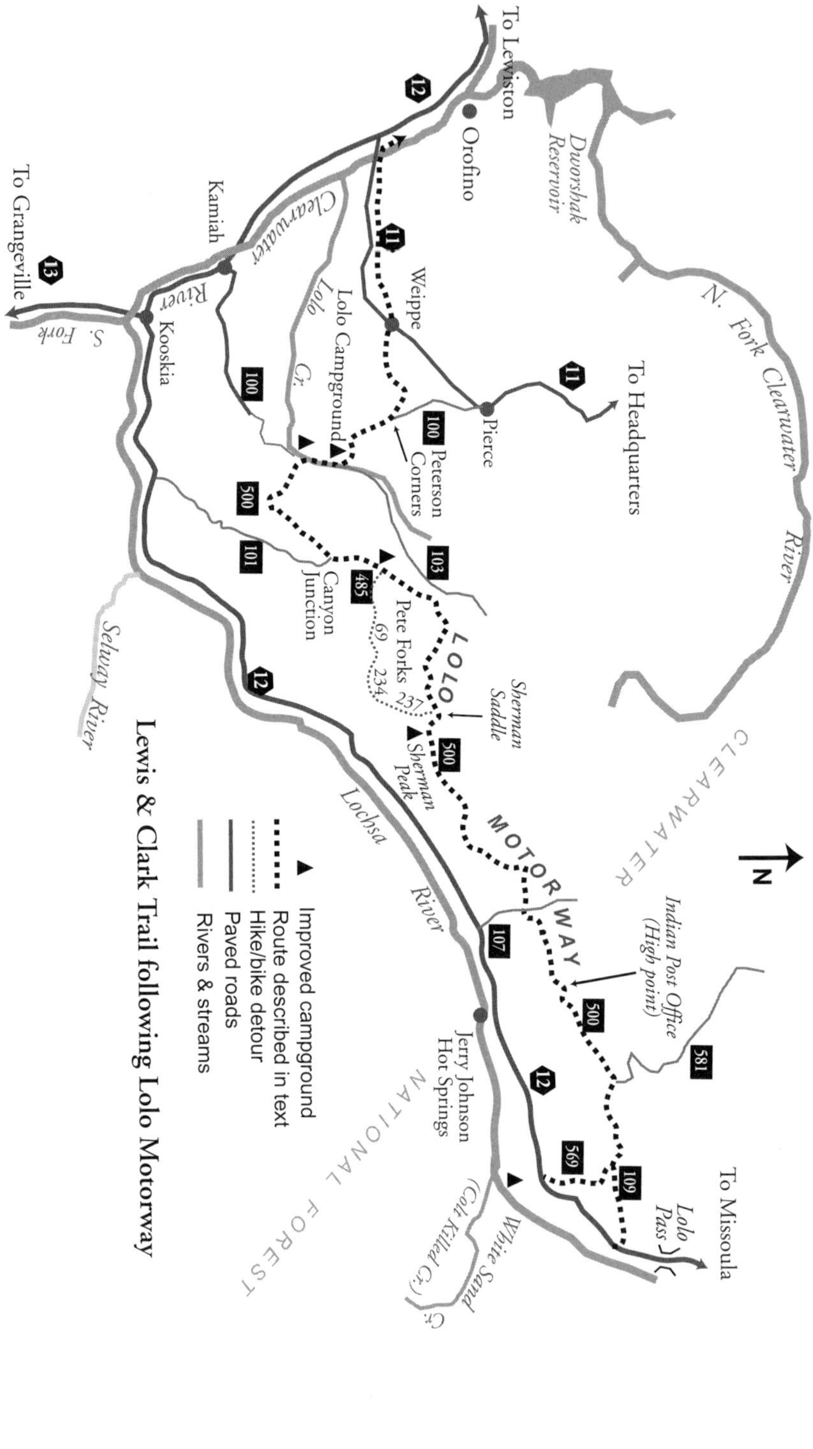

Lewis & Clark Trail following Lolo Motorway

party set off down the Clearwater to meet him at a fishing village. The place where the meeting took place is about a half mile east of the Weippe cemetery, about a half mile south of the town of Weippe. Hearing from the Nez Perce that the waters were navigable all the way to the ocean was a huge relief and lift for the expedition.

On September 24 the party traveled down to the Clearwater River until they found a suitable spot to fall trees and build canoes. This was near Chief Twisted Hair's camp, just a mile downstream from present day Orofino. On Highway 12 that spot is marked with a roadside historical sign, and it's called Canoe Camp. Here, until October 6, the expedition members were busy building the five craft that would carry them to the Pacific. The weather was warm and sunny, quite a contrast from the snow and cold they had just escaped. In ten days they had descended from 7,000 feet elevation to little more than 700. Although the expedition members all suffered terrible bouts of gastro-intestinal distress, they gathered strength and confidence.

On October 7, 1805, accompanied by Twisted Hair and Tetoharsky as guides, the expedition set off down the Clearwater in the new canoes. At this point, it's unclear exactly what happened, but it seems that Toby and his son, afraid of confronting the captains to leave the party, slipped away at night, taking two horses as payment for their services. The river ran true and clear, and despite the occasional whitewater rapids, they were able to make thirty, even forty miles a day. They left their horses with the Nez Perce for safe keeping over the winter, planning to pick them up on the journey home.

At the present location of Lewiston, Idaho, is the confluence of the Clearwater and Snake Rivers. Lewis first saw the Snake October 10, 1805, where they camped on the north side. It was originally named Lewis's River, and he thought it was the mighty Columbia. They actually reached the Columbia less than a week later after a float through hot desert country.

On their return trip to St. Louis in the early spring of 1806, Lewis and Clark spent almost a month with the Nez Perce on the Clearwater River. Having retrieved the horses the Nez Perce had faithfully kept for them over the winter while they were on the coast, they attempted to cross the Bitterroots. They were forced back by the deep snow. Finally, anxious to return home, and after two weeks wait for the snow to subside, the Corps of Discovery was able to cross the Bitterroots and return east.

Significance: The explorers were impressed by the honesty of the Nez Perce and ingenuity of the natives in using the natural resources about them. The expedition may not have succeeded without help from these people. Nowhere else on the entire trip did the explorers meet with such benevolence and assistance and in a time and place when perhaps they needed it the most.

If You Want to Go

Following Lewis and Clark's trail through Idaho from the Montana side, you can start about twenty miles south of Dillon, Montana, on I-15. Take Exit 44, which leads to Forest Road 324, heading west. FR 324 crosses the Beaverhead River and winds around the northern side of Clark Canyon Reservoir. Camp Fortunate lies beneath the reservoir now. A Lewis and Clark memorial park is on the northwest end of the water, and FR 324 passes right by it. Pass through the little town of Grant, and then about eight miles farther, go right as the road splits and up to Lemhi Pass. FR 324 goes left here and up over Bannack Pass, which is even higher, and it's a bit better road.

Martin Potucek photo

Trapper Peak from the Bitterroot Valley, on the Lewis and Clark route.

Caution! You don't need a four-wheel-drive, but be careful going over the pass. It can snow any time of the year up here. Large motorhomes or trailers should not attempt Lemhi Pass. The road up the east side is a relatively gentle grade, following Trail Creek, but gets steeper coming down the Idaho side.

Near the top of the pass on the east side is the Sacajewea Memorial Camp; it's a fine picnic site, but will be closed to camping. Just over the top of the pass, an interesting detour for the adventurous is Warm Springs Road (Forest Road 185), which heads off north. It follows the west side of the ridge, then winds around into the source of Pattee Creek. Following it will bring you by Sharkey Hot Spring, and farther down, near the junction with Old Highway 28 above the town of Tendoy (now, just a store), to the Fort Lemhi monument (an old Mormon fort), and by Pattee Creek, the Sacajewea Monument. This detour is dirt and rock, and a high ground clearance vehicle is advised. It's even appropriate for a bike loop that's mostly downhill to Tendoy.

Most folks will want to stick to the main route to Tendoy, down the Lewis and Clark Motorway, which mostly follows Agency Creek as it descends to the Lemhi River. Just east of Highway 28, and just after crossing Agency Creek, you can go right (north) on old Highway 28 (gravel) by Fort Lemhi and regain Highway 28 ten miles north. Take Highway 28 north (right) to continue following the 1805 expedition. Note: Just south (left) is a new BLM interpretive site on a small knoll. It shows where the expedition spent three days with Cameahwaite's band feasting and trading.

Heading north on Highway 28, it's about twenty miles to the town of Salmon. From Tendoy, you can also follow Old Highway 28 all the way to Salmon, which follows Lewis and Clark's trail more closely. Just south of Salmon, look for the new Sacajewea interpretive center, built for the wave of tourists expected for the Lewis and Clark bicentennial in 2003 to 2006.

At Salmon, follow U.S. 93 north; this is also where the Lemhi joins the Salmon River, which flows north until the town of North Fork. There it turns west toward the River of No Return Canyon. That's where Clark and a small party detoured five days unsuccessfully scouting a water route through the mountains. North Fork is also where the North Fork of the Salmon dumps into the main Salmon. Follow Highway 93 as it follows the North Fork north about three miles. Forest Road 91 heading west (left) is where one fork of the old South Nez Perce Trail joins the upper Salmon River Valley. It follows Hughes Creek up to the Bitterroot divide; this was an option for Lewis and Clark, rather than going up over Lost Trail. Whether they knew of this option is speculation.

Martin Potucek photo
Lolo Hot Springs as it is today.

In about another twenty miles, climb up over Lost Trail Pass at elevation 6,995 feet and enter Montana. The name comes from the 1805 crossing where Toby supposedly got confused. An interesting stop just over the pass is Lost Trail Hot Springs Resort. Now plunge down into the upper Bitterroot Valley. A little more than ten miles beyond the pass the junction/store of Sula (there's also a ranger station nearby) marks the area known then as Ross Hole. This is where the expedition traded for more horses and camped with the Flatheads.

Proceed north following the Bitterroot River. Just south of Darby Forest Road 473 heads west on another fork of the South Nez Perce Trail; the Magruder Corridor also follows this route. That was another option for the Corps of Discovery, but to resume our route, continue north to Hamilton on Highway 93 and to the town of Lolo where Traveler's Rest site can be found. At Lolo, go left (west) on U.S. 12, which follows Lolo Creek. About ten miles north lies the university town of Missoula, if you want to experience one of Montana's finest communities, including the University of Montana.

Not far out of Lolo you'll find Fort Fizzle historical site. This was where whites tried to stop the Nez Perce in their flight from General Howard in 1877. The significance here is that this is the eastern end of the ancient Lolo Trail, used by the Nez Perce and other tribes for generations to cross the Bitterroots from the west to access the buffalo hunting grounds of western Montana and beyond.

About seven miles before Lolo Pass come to Lolo Hot Springs where Clark found the water bubbling up from some rocks "hot and not bad tasting." Now you'll find a modest year-round resort with rooms, a restaurant, and warm and hot pools. Interesting granite hoodoos tower above the pools and in scattered locations across this open valley.

At Lolo Pass, there's a new visitor's center under construction, with plans for tours and lots of information on the Lewis and Clark Motorway. You can get to Packer Meadows (where the party camped September 13) by taking Forest Road 373 east a couple of miles; it can be found just south of the visitor's center. The easiest, most direct way to proceed from here is to follow U.S. 12 down the Lochsa River canyon to Kooskia. For the more adventurous, and to follow more accurately the expedition's footsteps, you can take the Lolo Motorway (Forest Road 500); more details on that route follow below.

Proceed west on 12 to the Powell Ranger Station; this is where the Corps of Discovery spent the night of September 14, 1805, on the Lochsa River. There is a great campground here with knowledgeable rangers. There are also cabins to rent, gas, and a small store. The newly rebuilt Lochsa Lodge replaces the old lodge that burned down in 2001. The new log structure displays excellent design and craftsmanship, and the restaurant it houses serves homemade and traditional American fare. Keep in mind that the next services, heading west, are seventy miles or more. If you stick to Highway 12, just follow it all the way to its

Martin Potucek photo
A new visitor center at Lolo Pass will be ready for the crowds of travelers expected during the Lewis and Clark Bicentennial.

junction with U.S. 95, which leads west to Lewiston, where Lewis and Clark left Idaho via the Snake River to the Columbia, and then to the Pacific.

To Follow the Lolo Motorway (Forest Road 500)

Note: This a rugged stretch of road, and should be taken only by those prepared for it. No services exist for more than 100 miles. Average vehicle speed is about fifteen mph; pavement to pavement is almost ninety miles. Check with the Forest Service at Powell or Lolo Pass before attempting it. Permits will be required to travel the Lolo Motorway during the bicentennial (2003-2006), and they will be limited. Travel will only be allowed east to west, initially. And note that it's only passable between mid-July and September most years. Be aware that even in summer, storms that bring rain can make sections of FR 500 extremely slick due to the clayey nature of the soil. Four-

Martin Potucek photo

Rocky Ridge Lake looking north from FR 500 (Lolo Motorway).

wheel-drive vehicles are not necessary, but low-clearance vehicles, including motorhomes and trailers, should not attempt this route.

The route described here comes out at Lolo Creek Road (FR 100). That leads north to Weippe (where Clark first came out of the mountains and met the Nez Perce). Mileages given are from the intersection of U.S. 12 and FR 569 where you turn off the pavement, so set your odometers to zero when you pass the Parachute Hill Road sign. (You can also access FR 500 via FR 109 back up toward Lolo Pass at a wide chain-up area with a call-box on U.S. 12; that road connects with our described route at Papoose Saddle or connects with FR 569 via Rocky Point.)

About a quarter mile east of the Powell turnoff, turn north off Highway 12 onto Forest Road 569; it's also marked as Parachute Hill Road. At 2.5 miles stay to middle of three-way split. At five miles you'll come to Powell

Martin Potucek photo

Looking south over Wendover Ridge on the Lolo Motorway.

Junction; go left onto FR 500. Just beyond is a sign marking Thirteen Mile Camp, where a foot trail leads to the site in one-third mile. At Papoose Saddle in a bit more than another mile stay to FR 500. FR 592 crosses here.

At 13 miles you'll find the site of the party's Snowbank Camp. It's on the right (north) side of the road and is marked. Wendover Ridge comes up from the south (Trail 85). This is where the expedition had to climb this grueling ridge after getting off route and following the Lochsa until it was impassable.

FR 500 now descends north to Cayuse Junction at 17.4 miles; Cayuse Lake is visible just north and below. The road then climbs steeply as the original trail cuts south of the road and follows the ridge. The road winds south and around a shoulder to a signboard reading: Bear Oil & Roots at mile twenty-one.

Mile 24 brings you to a saddle and junction with Forest Road 566 that goes left and south down to Highway 12.

This is a good road to bail out on for comfort or emergencies.

Indian Post Office is at mile 25.8; here you'll find rock cairns put up by whites, which were supposedly used to pass messages. At almost 7,000 feet elevation, you've passed the highest spot on the Lolo Motorway about a mile back. Note that at Indian Post Office the Corps' route goes north of FR 500 dropping down to follow Moon and then Howard Creeks and doesn't meet up again with FR 500 until another eight miles west. At almost twenty-eight miles, dip through Moon Saddle where the Nez Perce (Lolo) Trail crosses the road, briefly, back to the north.

At 30.3 miles you come to Howard Camp (after General Howard in the 1877 campaign) and a road running north (FR 588) to Horseshoe Lake. Devil's Chair, an interesting granite formation, is found at 31.7.

Mile 33.7 brings you to the junction of FR 107, where going left (south) brings you back to U.S. 12, another point to bail out. This is also marked as Saddle Camp; 107 also goes right (north) to Cayuse Creek.

Following the Lolo Motorway west brings you to Twelve Mile Saddle at thirty-seven miles where 500 winds around the north side of Indian Grave Peak. Sinque Hole Camp can be reached by a foot trail just east and a bit north of the peak. It's a good trail (Trail 1965) to hike the original trail a couple of miles and meet your vehicle just south of Indian Grave Peak if someone is willing to shuttle it forward. It comes out at The Smoking Place sign (mile thirty-nine).

The trail now heads south and, at 44.2 miles, to Greensward Camp on Bald Mountain where the forest opens up to wide grassy slopes. At 46.3 the lodgepole pines crowd in to Dry Camp, but there's still a nice view south.

Martin Potucek photo

Lochsa River at Powell, Idaho.

Spirit Revival Ridge on Sherman Peak at 49 miles is named after the place where the captains first caught a glimpse of the meadows at Weippe (and the end of the mountains). The road then goes around the north side of Chimney Butte through Sherman Saddle (mile 51.6), while the expedition's route leads around the south side and through Horse Sweat Pass.

At just over fifty-three miles the Corps of Discovery's trail goes south down Willow Ridge on Trail 237. This trail goes down to Hungery Creek and other camps of the expedition and comes out west at Pete Forks. **Warning!** This is a gnarly trail that goes through extreme terrain. Brush on Trail 69P, which connects 237 to Pete Forks along Hungery Creek, grows like kudzu in Alabama. People have been lost in here. Do not attempt to hike down into this drainage unless you are an expert in trail skills and have made serious preparations!

At miles 54.8 and 58 drop down and climb out of Deep Saddle and Green Saddle, respectively. 60.2 brings you to Weitas Meadows on the left (south). A half mile beyond is Weitas Butte Lookout Road (FR 557) to the right (north), which is an interesting bike detour. Just beyond is another road going right that drops down to Rocky Ridge Lake and campground; this is a great spot to overnight while exploring the trails.

At 65.6 come to a junction where Forest Road 104 goes right (north). Stay to the main route and left. This is rather confusing because, at this writing, there was no sign (or if there was, we didn't find it) identifying it. On USGS topo maps it is marked as Pete Forks. Pete Forks and campground are marked (on the Clearwater National Forest map) as what's signed on the trail as Boundary Junction. For the purposes of this book, when there's a conflict, I will go with what's on site.

At 68.2 miles stay right to FR 500 at a fork known as Boundary Junction. FR 485 goes left to Windy Saddle and Boundary Peak; that's also where the Corps came out of Hungery Creek.

At seventy-four miles you arrive at Canyon Junction, and it can be confusing due to the three roads that come together here. Stay right (west) to FR 500, which turns to a wide gravel roadbed now. (Going straight through Canyon Junction on FR 101 will lead you back to U.S. 12 on the Clearwater River upstream from Kooskia, but it's a long and winding road.) A couple miles farther the expedition's route again leaves FR 500 at Small Prairie Camp where it veers north over Eldorado Ridge and then drops down into Lolo Creek (the Idaho Lolo Creek). 500 loops south around Eldorado Ridge and ends up at the same spot: near Pheasant Camp and at the Lolo Creek Campground where FR 500 meets FR 100.

Martin Potucek photo

Where Lewis and Clark made contact with the Nez Perces, south of Weippe.

At mile 79.6 pass Small Prairie Camp site as the road follows Eldorado Creek. In almost another three miles Forest Road 500 swings back north. At 85.5 miles FR 520 goes off right; by taking this detour about 1.5 miles, you'll find Lewis and Clark Grove Camp, a beautiful cedar grove on the explorer's route.

At almost 87 miles you come to FR 100 (pavement) and the official end of FR 500, the Lolo Motorway. From this junction on Lolo Creek you can go either of two ways. South (left) on FR 100 takes you to U.S. 12 just north of Kamiah to the Long Camp site where the expedition spent three weeks with the Nez Perce waiting for the snows to subside in late spring of 1806. End Lolo Motorway section.

If you go right on Forest Road 100, don't miss the Bradford Bridge site and sign (north from the junction a few hundred yards), the site where the Corps crossed Lolo

Creek (no bridge then, of course). FR 5112 (accessed from the bridge) follows the Corps' route west more closely to the Weippe Prairie, but the unmarked roads are difficult and confusing. Our motor route north (right from the junction of FR 500 and 100) takes you up Lolo Creek, then veers west at Musselshell Meadow to Brown Creek. A few miles farther, at Peterson Corners, go left (west) on Mussellshell Road and leave FR 100, which heads north to Pierce. In eight miles this brings you to the town of Weippe.

If you want to visit the site where Clark first met the Nez Perce, go left (south) on Cemetery Road; it's paved and just east of the school in Weippe. Go south about two miles on Cemetery Road, passing the cemetery to the left. Then go left (east) on Larson Road about one-half mile. A signboard marks the site.

Following Idaho Highway 11 (yes, you're back on pavement again) about fifteen miles west brings you through Greer to U.S. 12 a half dozen miles south of Orofino on the Clearwater River. Travel north and west on U.S. 12. About four miles west of Orofino brings you to a place where the North Fork joins the main Clearwater River. On the north side of the river lies the town of Ahsahka, while on the south can be found Canoe Camp where the expedition spent ten days building the canoes that would take them to the Pacific.

Follow U.S. 12 west to where it meets U.S. 95. Both highways share the same route following the north bank of the Clearwater to Lewiston, Idaho. From Canoe Camp the Corps made great progress, sometimes thirty or forty miles a day. The route from present-day Lewiston follows the Snake and the Columbia Rivers all the way to the goal, the Pacific coast of the continent.

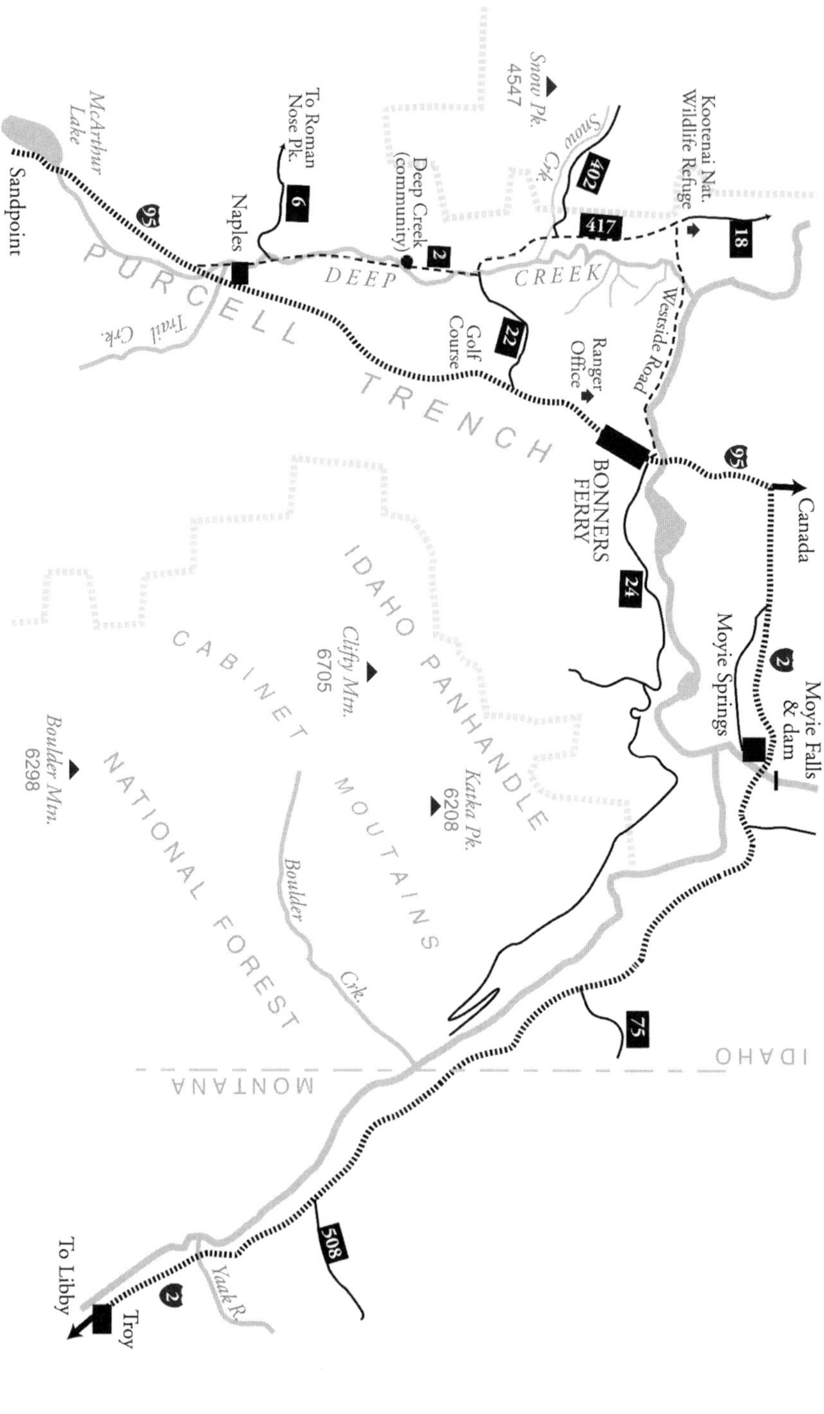
Sandpoint
McArthur Lake
95
Naples
To Roman Nose Pk.
6
Deep Creek (community)
2
Snow Pk. 4547
Snow Crk.
402
417
Kootenai Nat. Wildlife Refuge
18
DEEP CREEK
PURCELL TRENCH
Trail Crk.
Golf Course
22
Ranger Office
Westside Road
BONNERS FERRY
95
Canada
24
IDAHO PANHANDLE
CABINET MOUTAINS
NATIONAL FOREST
Clifty Mtn. 6705
Katka Pk. 6208
Boulder Mtn. 6298
Boulder Crk.
Moyie Springs
Moyie Falls & dam
2
75
IDAHO
MONTANA
508
Yaak R.
2
Troy
To Libby

Chapter Two

DAVID THOMPSON AND KULLYSPELL HOUSE

Born in Westminster, England, April 30, 1770, David Thompson's mother moved his family to London before he was two years old, just after his father's death. Showing great aptitude for math and science, he was enrolled in a school that helped train navigators for the Royal Navy and merchants.

After Britain and the new United States signed the peace treaty of 1783 Thompson was sent to a Hudson's Bay Co. fur outpost at Churchill on Hudson's Bay in northern Ontario. In 1797, at the age of twenty-seven, while exploring and mapping fur trade routes in Saskatchewan, he met Alexander Fraser, who hired him away from Hudson's Bay Company and into the North West Company, Hudson's chief competitor.

Armed with scientific instruments such as the sextant, telescope, barometer, chronometer, compass, and thermometer, he had a natural and intense curiosity about the world. This suited him perfectly to become an explorer and mapmaker for the unknown and uncharted lands of the Pacific Northwest at the turn of the eighteenth century.

More than just charting the rivers and mountains of the new lands, he also kept wonderful observations of the birds, wildlife, and curiosities of the native people he encountered.

After an initial expedition west with James Hughes in 1801, he returned to Rocky Mountain House, an outpost on the Saskatchewan River. They failed to find a passage through the Rocky Mountains, over the continental divide, and onto the Columbia River that would eventually lead to the Pacific Ocean.

In the spring of 1807, after following a track over Howse Pass and down Blaeberry Creek to the Columbia River, he discovered Columbia Lake, the headwaters of the Columbia River. His group had crossed the divide, what they had failed to do on his first attempt. At the time he did not realize that from that lake, all that was needed to reach the Pacific, was to follow it downstream. He established a fur trading outpost (built like a fort to resist attacks by the warlike Piegans) on the upper Columbia above Windermere, B.C. The post was called Kootenay House, and it was the first commercial establishment west of the Rockies in either the U.S. or Canada.

In July 1809 Thompson began his third adventure west with seven other men in his party. Setting out from Fort Augustus near present day Edmonton, Alberta, this was Thompson's first trip as a commercial venture. His purpose this time, rather than exploring and mapping, was to establish a trading post for the North West Company farther into the Columbia River region.

From the Columbia River his party portaged over Canal Flats to the Kootenai River. With help from some Flatheads, the party was able to portage around Kootenai Falls between Libby and Troy, Montana. An outpost may have been established near present day Leonia, Idaho, on the Idaho-Montana border. This part of the Kootenai is

Martin Potucek photo

A view of the Kootenai River looking west toward Bonners Ferry. The Selkirk Mountains are in the background.

marked by rocky cliffs and steep overhanging hillsides, but is surprisingly navigable.

Thompson then floated the Kootenai River downstream to the location of present Bonners Ferry, Idaho. Here, the Kootenai opens up into a broad, lush valley, after sweeping around the northern end of the Cabinet Mountain Range. To Thompson's frustration, it can only be surmised, the river turned from a northwest direction here to almost due north as it slowed in oxbow fashion. Finan McDonald was sent to bring Indian guides and help with horses. It was here in this broad valley they would leave the water again to travel overland south, and hopefully west.

Their overland route south down the Purcell Trench toward Lake Pend Oreille followed Deep Creek (which flows north) to a small divide and down Sand Creek (which flows south). This portion of the route Thompson noted in his journals as the Lake Indian Road. It was an ancient thoroughfare that is mostly level with good forage for the animals, and with plenty of water in the form of many small lakes and streams. In most places the two-day journey between the Kootenai and Pend Oreille did not follow a single track. The broad, probably overgrown trail took many different tracks except in places like Elmira where the mountains squeezed the broad corridor down to a narrow defile.

Thompson noted in his journal on September 8, 1809, that the place where Sand Creek joined Lake Pend Oreille (pronounced pondeRAY) looked like a "point of sand," thus the name now given to present day Sandpoint, Idaho.

Sending the horses around the north end of Lake Pend Oreille, Thompson paddled east across the lake to the mouth of what he called the Clark's Fork (of the Columbia) River the next day. This is now called the Clark Fork River that winds its way southeast through rock-walled canyons with only intermittent rapids to deter canoe travel. The name was to honor William Clark, of Lewis and Clark fame, for the great achievement of the 1803-06 expedition. Just east two days' paddle, between present day Thompson Falls, Montana, and the aptly named Thompson River, he later established Saleesh House—another fur trading post for the North West Company.

For the next few days Thompson scouted the area, searching for a suitable location for a fur trading outpost. On September 11, 1809, he chose a point of land on the lake's northeastern shore just across from what's now Memaloose Island. His men erected a high scaffolding to protect their stores until a storehouse could be built. On September 23, his men finished building a log storehouse. A log house was started two weeks later; Thompson called it Kullyspell House, after the Kalispel people who lived around the lake. It was an excellent location for a trade

Martin Potucek photo
Kullyspell House site. Memaloose Island can be seen in the background.

post; it sat on a protected point of land that canoe parties would pass on their paddle across the northern end of Lake Pend Oreille. That was the big water connecting the Clark Fork (and the buffalo country of western Montana) to the Columbia River (and the Pacific Ocean).

Trade with the Indians began almost immediately. At the mouth of the Clark Fork River, just a few miles east, the traders located a camp mostly of Kalispels (Flatheads) but there were also Spokanes and Kootenais, numbering around eighty. The Piegans (a branch of the Blackfeet) were their ancestral enemies, and had received guns from traders east of the divide, so these people were eager to get the new weaponry themselves. At the time, even pieces of iron (to forge arrowheads and other implements) were of great value to the native people. Thompson was familiar with the Piegans, had learned their language and had lived with them, and he knew of their tradition of raiding

Martin Potucek photo

Kootenai River trail.

their neighbors. One source says he brought guns on this first trip to trade to the natives for furs. Perhaps Thompson saw this leveling of the play field as having a stabilizing effect. It's possible the introduction of firearms may have happened at some subsequent time and place. It's unlikely the mapmaker would have carried such a cargo in 1809 on his first trip to Pend Oreille country.

Earlier maps of the area, which were quite sketchy, showed the river flowing out of Pend Oreille (the largest lake in Idaho and the deepest in the U.S.) as the Clark Fork. Thompson called it the Saleesh (The entire region's native population and language group is known as Salish or Salishan). So, it was considered the same river flowing in and out of this body of water at the time. Now, named after the pendants worn from the ears of the native people there, it was called Pend Oreille (pierced ear) River.

Getting the lay of the land from local Kalispels, and accompanied by a local youngster, Thompson set off on

September 27, 1809, with one of his men downstream on the Pend Oreille River. Crossing to the northwest side of the lake at Sandpoint, then following the river to pass the mouth of Priest River near the Pend Oreille River, he passed what's now Albeni Falls and into present day Washington state. This was about fifty miles west of Kullyspell House.

He turned around before reaching Box Canyon on October 3, and we're not sure why. Still looking for the main Columbia River that would serve as future highway to the Pacific, he did not realize that only another day's journey by land from this point would bring him to it. Some think that he was unnerved by the northerly direction of the river's flow, for he knew he had to go west to the ocean.

The next year Thompson retraced his steps, but once again, he turned back, this time at Box Canyon. On October 6 he returned to Kullyspell House where trading with the Indians was going well; 200 lbs. of furs had already been gathered, and word was spreading to others. Thompson's main concern was finding the western route, not commercial enterprise, which some say, he was never really interested in.

In 1810 Thompson traveled west from near present day Cusick, Washington, overland through a string of small lakes to the confluence of the Spokane and Little Spokane Rivers. This is called the Kalispell Trail. At that confluence Thompson established Spokane House for the North West Company. Shortly after that, John Jacob Astor's American enterprise would set up at nearby Fort Spokane. These outposts would become the economic basis for the future of modern Spokane, Washington.

Early in 1811, Thompson led a party over Athabasca Pass east of the Columbia's northermost reach. From there, he gained the Wood River, which led him to the

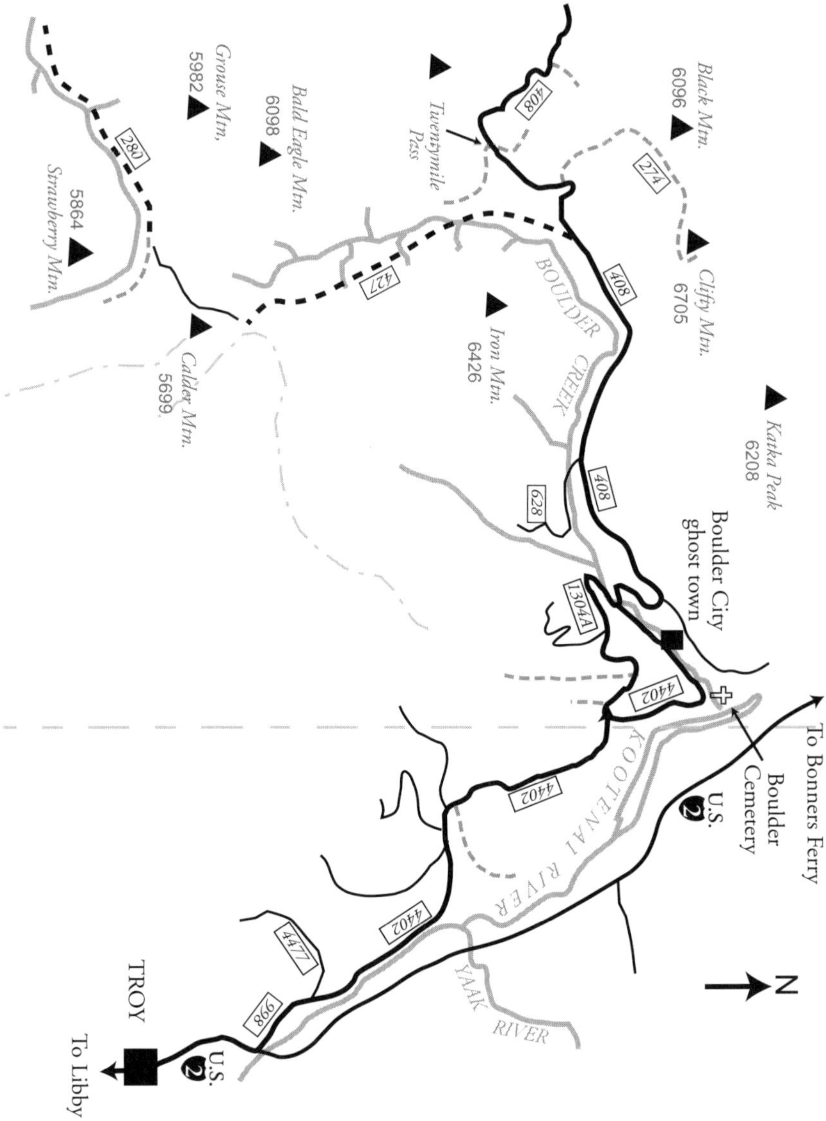
Black Mtn.
6096
Twentymile Pass
Bald Eagle Mtn.
6098
Grouse Mtn.
5982
Strawberry Mtn.
5864
Clifty Mtn.
6705
Iron Mtn.
6426
Calder Mtn.
5699
Katka Peak
6208
BOULDER CREEK
Boulder City ghost town
Boulder Cemetery
To Bonners Ferry
KOOTENAI RIVER
YAAK RIVER
U.S. 2
N
TROY
To Libby
408
274
280
427
628
1304A
4402
4477
998

Columbia itself. Racing the Astorians to the Pacific, he reached that goal by following the Columbia all the way to its mouth. He arrived there July 15, 1811, only to find that the Americans had beat him there by four months and had established their post at Astoria, Oregon.

David Thompson was a true explorer; he became the first European to traverse the entire Columbia River and to survey it completely, from source to sea. He established trading posts and routes across present day Canada, Idaho, Washington, Oregon and Montana. Perhaps his greatest achievements were the maps he created of the rivers and mountains he explored. Some were used into the twentieth century, and they laid the groundwork for others to follow. From the Great Lakes to the Pacific Ocean, his adventures helped to open the Pacific Northwest.

If You Want to Go

Begin tracing David Thompson's journey across Idaho to establish Kullyspell House by starting at Troy, Montana, on U.S. Highway 2. If you'd like current maps or information, stop by the U.S. Forest Service ranger station about a mile west of Troy.

Adventure Detour: Some sources suggest that David Thompson did not follow the Kootenai River downstream all the way to present-day Bonners Ferry, but that he took horses south up Boulder Creek drainage, over a divide just east of the Cabinet Mountains crest, and then down into the Grouse Creek drainage. West of Troy, Montana, this route follows Forest Road 998, turns into 4402, and then above Boulder City, follows FR 408 to come out on U.S. Highway 95 near Naples, Idaho. Beware that the middle section of 408, where it sweeps north along Boulder Creek, is marginal at best, and may be unpassable. Forest Road 427 also forks south off of 408 to follow Boulder Creek most of the way to the Cabinet Crest where trails (67 and 488) lead south and west to Grouse Creek and FR 280. Anyone attempting to follow this speculative route should check local trail and road conditions. End of detour.

Resuming our main motor route, follow U.S. 2 west of Troy where it crosses to the north side of the Kootenai River. The river makes a turn to the north just east of Troy and continues in a northwestern direction until well into Idaho, so you're also following the eastern banks of the river. The river in many places is not visible from the highway due to the steep rock walls just above it. A nice campground at the confluence of the Yaak and Kootenai Rivers is a good place to contemplate the outpost that Finan McDonald may have set up here almost 200 years ago.

Continue on U.S. Highway 2 west through Leonia where we enter Idaho. It's another ten miles or so to the bridge over the Moyie River Canyon; it's worth a stop to view this spectacular gorge. Excellent trout fishing and Class 5 whitewater can be found seasonably up this scenic canyon to the north. Continue on U.S. 2 west another six miles to the junction with U.S. 95 where you go left and south to follow David Thompson's main route to Bonners Ferry, Idaho.

Most historians believe David Thompson canoed the Kootenai River downstream to Bonners Ferry. The Kootenai, as other rivers in this region, does not flow in a consistent direction; it has the peculiarity of flowing down out of Canada, into the U.S., then back north again, and then finally into what we now call the main Columbia River by Trail, British Columbia.

To follow the main route from Bonners Ferry, go left on U.S. Highway 95 and south to Sandpoint. On your way out of Bonners Ferry, heading south, you'll pass the Bonners Ferry Ranger District office, so stop in for info or maps. On your way up the highway grade just south and overlooking the Mirror Lake Golf Course, there are three highway signboards, and one of them is about David Thompson.

Martin Potucek photo

Kootenai River at start of FR 24.

Near Elmira, just south of McArthur Lake, we cross the divide between the Kootenai and the Pend Oreille Rivers. The Selkirk Mountain Range just west of the highway forms a near-continuous massif from Sandpoint, just twenty-five miles south to almost 200 miles north into British Columbia. At Naples, to the west you'll see Roman Nose, a local landmark projecting more than 7,000 ft. elevation, as do the "Sisters" peaks (the Selkirk Crest) if you look west from Colburn, farther south.

To continue on Thompson's route to Kullyspell House, go left (east) on Idaho 200 as it leaves US 95 about a half mile north of Sandpoint. The body of water to the south side of this intersection is the estuary of Sand Creek before it flows into Lake Pend Oreille. It's near this point where Thompson named this place a "point of sand."

Proceed on 200 east for about fifteen miles to the town of Hope where a roadside historical marker notes Thompson's journey. At another 2.5 miles east, turn right onto Penninsula Road that leads to the Samowen Campground. It's near the end of this road that the most likely spot of Kullyspell House is located. Unfortunately for the public, the site is on private property and is not accessible. Private homes block access to the lakeshore. The entire peninsula is a game preserve (named after David Thompson), so you'll see plenty of deer and wild turkeys. Near the end of Kullyspell Drive you can look out and see Memaloose Island, a quarter mile long splinter of rock and trees just 100 yards offshore. At the point of land just opposite this island is the site of Kullyspell House.

Chapter Three

THE OREGON TRAIL

After Lewis and Clark's Corps of Discovery returned to St. Louis in 1806, the ambitions of American expansionists and settlers grew bolder and more organized. Fur traders followed Indian trails west as the demand for beaver pelts rose.

By the 1840s the western mid-latitudes of the North American continent were a vast and unexplored frontier that was far from America's borders. While the Louisiana Purchase of 1803 added the land between the Mississippi River and the Rocky Mountains from the French, that region was unmapped, unsettled, and unknown. Spain controlled California through its system of missions and ranchos, and Britain's influence over the Northwest seemed to be consolidating through its Hudson's Bay Company posts and network of trappers.

In 1839 the worst economic downturn of the century began and would continue into the 1850s. Agricultural markets failed over most of the country, and especially at

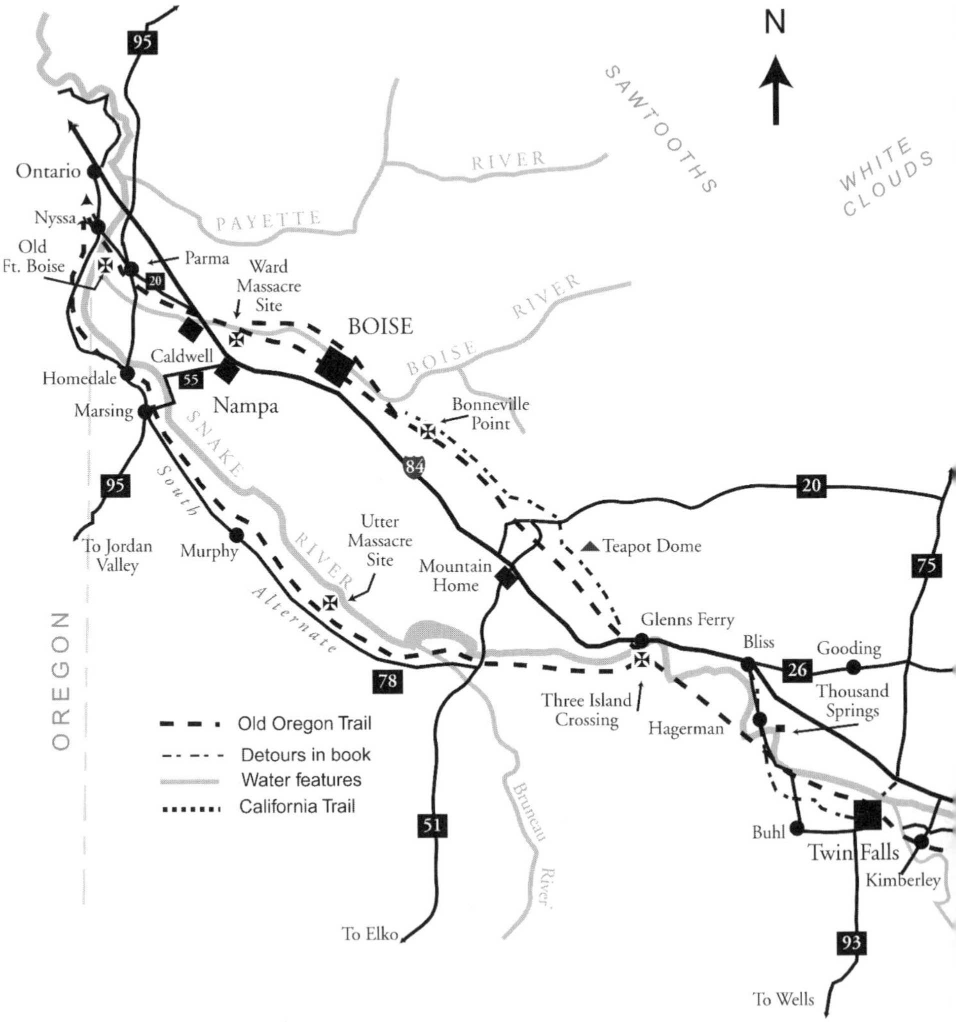
N
SAWTOOTHS
WHITE CLOUDS
PAYETTE RIVER
BOISE RIVER
SNAKE RIVER
South Alternate
Bruneau River
OREGON
Ontario
Nyssa
Old Ft. Boise
Parma
Ward Massacre Site
BOISE
Caldwell
Homedale
Marsing
Nampa
Bonneville Point
To Jordan Valley
Murphy
Utter Massacre Site
Mountain Home
Teapot Dome
Glenns Ferry
Bliss
Gooding
Three Island Crossing
Hagerman
Thousand Springs
Buhl
Twin Falls
Kimberley
To Elko
To Wells
95
20
55
84
78
51
26
75
93
Old Oregon Trail
Detours in book
Water features
California Trail

OREGON TRAIL IN IDAHO

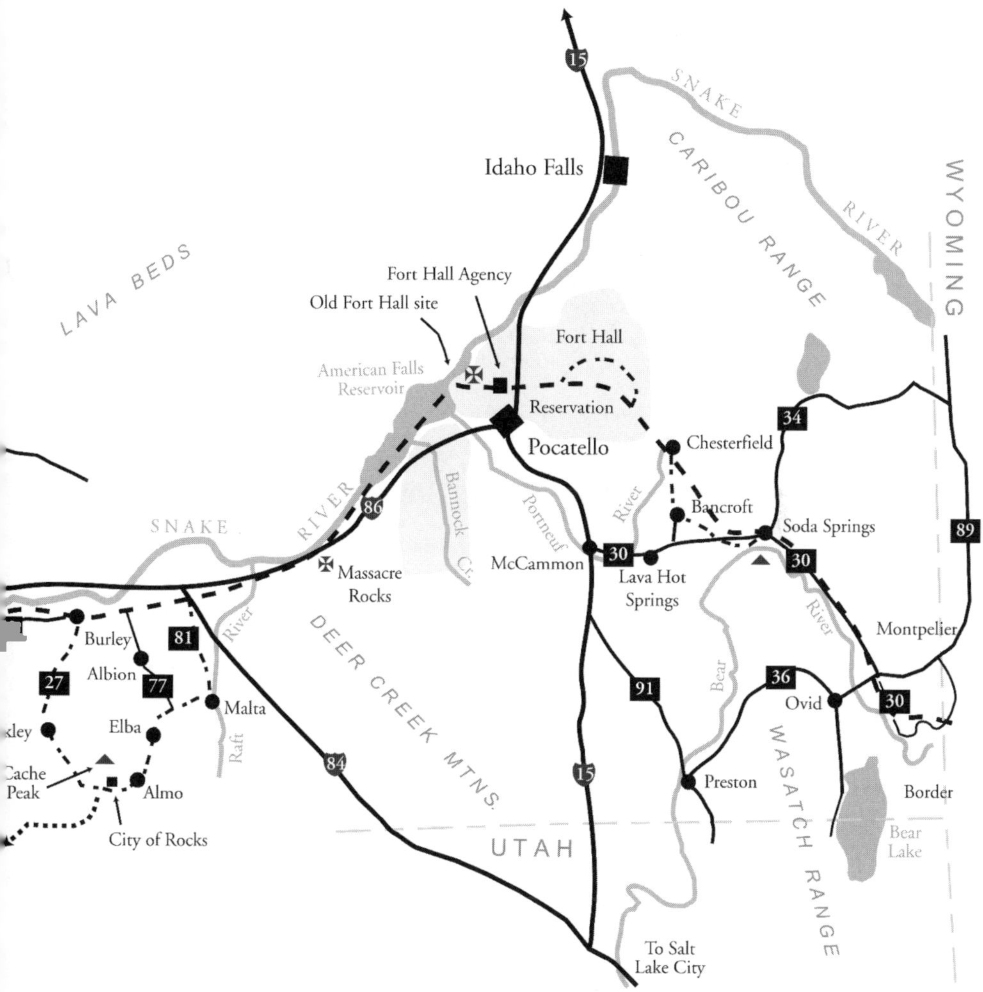

the western frontier, which was now at the Mississippi and Missouri rivers. People were losing land, farms, and businesses as few could afford to pay their debts. In early 1843 Senators Linn and Benton of Missouri sponsored a bill giving American pioneers who settled in Oregon country free land, a section for each pioneer and an additional 160 acres for each child in the family. The bill didn't become reality until 1850, but it stirred huge public interest. Senator Benton himself coined the term "Manifest Destiny" in describing Americans' duty to expand the nation to the Pacific.

Into this exploding world came a young New England doctor, Marcus Whitman and his new wife, Narcissa. They met through church society, and both were fervent in their faith. In 1836 they traveled with another church-sponsored couple, Henry and Eliza Spalding, to set up missions in the Northwest: their purpose—to minister the Christian faith to the native people there. That small expedition was significant as it followed a fur trapper's caravan west to one of the last summer mountain Rendezvous (a gathering of trappers and traders from all over the Rocky Mountain region to trade and resupply their endeavors). These were the first white women and the first wagon to reach Fort Hall, a Hudson's Bay Company outpost on the Snake River.

Perhaps the greater significance of that 1836 trip was the familiarity it gave Whitman. He would prove that the route over South Pass (the Continental Divide), down the Snake River Plain, and up over the Blue Mountains to the Columbia River was the best overland trail to Oregon. "Oregon" at the time meant the entire Pacific Northwest, but most emigrants were headed for the fertile Willamette Valley. This route, once proven that a sturdy wagon could make it, would open a trail that would funnel the tide of

American expansion.

The spring of 1843 brought several individuals and groups to Independence, Missouri. One was Marcus Whitman. The previous winter he set out solo from Walla Walla to cross the continent to Boston. His purpose was to persuade the board that controlled foreign church missions not to close his newly established outpost. Unrelated, Lieutenant John C. Fremont was preparing a survey expedition of forty men to map the Oregon and California Trails for the U.S. government.

Aside from the normal groups outfitted for hunting, trapping, and trading in the Rockies for the coming season, a new force was converging and amassing at and near Independence; it was a trickle of disparate parties in wagons headed west to stake their claims in Oregon. These were farm families mostly, some dispossessed—some restless, adventurers, dreamers, and wanderers. Whitman's timing couldn't have been better. He arrived at the seminal "jumping off" point just in time to head out with an advance party that would lead almost 900 people, over 100 wagons, and thousands of head of stock in the single largest, most ambitious expedition by settlers moving to the Oregon country. On May 21, 1843, the Oregon Emigrating Company, as it was organized and named, set out for what would later be called The Great Emigration of 1843.

The emigrants first came to what is now Idaho from Fort Bridger, a new fort on the Green River in Wyoming just constructed by the famous scout Jim Bridger and his partner Louis Vasquez. Surviving a section of barren ground, the travelers passed into present Idaho about a mile east of crossing a small tributary of the Bear River, called Thomas Fork. They then climbed a steep mountain later called Big Hill to descend into the Bear River. This

Martin Potucek photo
Soda Point/Sheep Rock near Soda Springs. The rocky point was a major landmark on the Oregon Trail.

was now lush and fertile land, and it gave their animals great nourishment after what they had come through. There was also an abundance of fish and waterfowl for the pioneers. Trout was a new treat for them, not found previously on the trip.

Following the Bear River northwestward, they came upon three sets of wondrous hot springs. First was Beer Springs, then Soda Springs, and finally a bit out of their way, Steamboat Springs, named after the periodic thumping and puffing it produced. Fremont's group caught up to the wagon train in this area.

Shoshoni/Bannock natives also paid the emigrants a visit. Accompanying the Indians was famed trapper Peg Leg Smith. Kit Carson, with Fremont, fascinated the pioneers with stories of his adventures with the Indians. In that respect, this big train was very fortunate; the local natives were mostly considered as friendly traders. Animosities would not arise until later growing herds and emigrants decimated area foodstocks and grasses.

The wagon train struck north as the Bear River made a big turn back south. It was about twenty miles to the next stream, the Portneuf River, which they gained by climbing a gentle divide north of present day Chesterfield. Crossing this divide now brought them into the Columbia River basin, and more immediately, to the Snake River and Fort Hall.

Fort Hall was originally an American enterprise started by Nathaniel Wyeth in 1834 to compete with Hudson's Bay Company and its dominance of the fur trade in the Northwest. Wyeth was able to hang on only a couple of years and then sold out to his competitors. When the emigrants arrived there on August 27, 1843, they were received hospitably by the outpost's leader, Richard Grant. Because this was the first train of anywhere near this size, the first few dozen wagons wiped out the Fort's stock of supplies. Anger grew as the trailing elements of the group found the fort's store had nothing to sell.

Fort Hall was a pivotal point for the emigrants for a number of reasons. For one, wagons had never before been taken west of this point on the trail (with the exception of Whitmans in 1836). This was also the last outpost for some 300 miles, until Fort Boise lower on the Snake River near Idaho's present border with Oregon.

The issue of whether wagons should continue or be left behind was paramount. Grant advised them not to even try, as it had never been done before, while Whitman urged everyone to proceed intact, not to leave their wagons, tools, and supplies. For Grant, it may have been more of a political imperative, as the U.S. and Britain were still contending for sovereignty over this part of the world. If a wagon road could be put through, America's claim to the land west would be greatly enhanced, if only for the increased number of settlers it would bring. Whitman was driven by his conviction that it was possible to drive a wagon all the way to the Columbia. (Joe Meek and Robert Newall succeeded in getting a two-wheeled version of his cart all the way over the Blue Mountains to his mission near Walla Walla in 1840.) He also was concerned that these pioneers would need everything they could carry once they reached their promised land.

Fort Hall was a badly needed resting-place for the emigrants. Although two-thirds of the journey was behind them, they needed to go another 600 miles or more to the Willamette River Valley, and the toughest section still lay before them. A week was spent at the fort repairing wagons and harnesses and washing and mending clothes. Counsels were made that week, and speeches were given; the main issue still was whether to proceed with wagons past Fort Hall. After much debate, most decided to take their wagons, so on September 3 the train proceeded westward, following the south bank of the Snake River.

"Following the south bank of the Snake River" may sound like an innocuous enough term, but for accuracy, a little topographical detail needs to given. In very few places between Fort Hall and Fort Boise does the Snake River gently slope down from its wide, arid plain to a riverbank. Mostly, a sharp-walled precipice drops between sixty and 200 vertical feet down to the water. For many a mile, the emigrants traveled a short distance from the river, but could not access the water due to the sheer basalt barrier. Not only that, but rocky ground and thick sage brush were constantly breaking down the wagons. The forgiving topsoil of the Great Plains east of Fort

Martin Potucek photo

Lava Hot Springs on the Oregon Trail motor route.

Bridger seemed like a highway compared to this. Afternoons, temperatures soared this time of year.

From Fort Hall the first obstacles crossed were the Portneuf River and then Bannock Creek. Another day's journey as the river turned southwest brought them to a fifty vertical foot cascade now known as American Falls (near where the present dam is located).

The next crossings were at Rock Creek and then the Raft River, which is little more than an irrigation ditch now. The Raft River crossing was significant not because of its size or difficulty, but because just beyond it is where the Martin and Chiles party, including fifteen wagons, split off south on a trail to California.

At Salmon Falls, they came across a large encampment of Indians, perhaps numbering in the hundreds. Everyone in the fishing village was occupied with catching salmon,

Martin Potucek photo

Register Rock at Massacre Rocks State Park, just off I-86.

cleaning and drying them, or transporting them. There was an abundance of fish and a willingness by the natives to trade the food to the pioneers for useful items, such as clothes and simple tools.

About thirty miles downstream the river spread into a wide bay, marked by three islands in midstream. This was where the wagons would cross the Snake, and they called it Island Crossing (later, Three Island Crossing). On September 11, by chaining the wagons together in groups of about ten, they were able to safely cross the river, all but one wagon and man. His name was Miles Eyres, and he refused to connect his wagon to others. The strong current, even at this time of low water, conspired to upset his wagon and team. He was never found, and although his wife and kids were spared by being on another wagon, because he carried all his money on him, his family was left destitute. They spent that next winter with the

Whitmans at Walla Walla.

It took almost three full days for the entire train to cross, but by September 13, rain started to fall. The river began to rise and a few wagons at the end of the train were not able to cross. These stragglers had little choice but to follow the river along its south bank where they would try to rejoin the train at Fort Boise. This detour would become known as the South Alternate, and in later years would be used by thousands of pioneers whom also, for one reason or another, did not cross the Snake at this crucial point. That alternate would also become known as the Dry Route, known for its rocks, dust, and lack of water. It rejoined the main Oregon Trail at Fort Boise, where the Boise River flows into the Snake.

On the second day after the crossing and heading northwest (see detour in If You Want to Go), the train came upon three small hot springs bubbling up out of a rock outcropping on a small creek. This was called Boiling Springs; later, John Newby called it Hot Springs Creek. The springs, a welcome curiosity, were right off the trail and just south of the landmark that would be known as Teapot Dome. The trail from here continued mostly west over patchy ground to a rise where the Boise River Valley could first be spotted. This place was later called Bonneville Point, for it's where Benjamin L. E. Bonneville is supposed to have spied the river and exclaimed, "les Bois, les Bois!"—the trees, the trees! Whether he did or not, it must have been a stirring sight to see a heavily wooded river after the previous 300 miles with little more to shelter under than wagons and sage.

Reaching the south bank of the Boise River on September 18, the emigrants pushed on west to Canyon Hill (in Caldwell) to cross to the north side of the Boise River. From here, it was an easy drive to Fort Boise. Like

Martin Potucek photo

Conestoga wagon exhibit at Three Island Crossing State Park.

Fort Hall, old Fort Boise was another Hudson's Bay Company outpost. This fortified fur trading post was located at the juncture of the Boise and Snake Rivers. A jovial and accommodating French fur trapper named Francois Payette ran the place. He became well-known for years to come for his hospitality and helpfulness to weary travelers.

Fort Boise was where all of the members of the main train that crossed the Snake at Island Crossing would now have to recross the river. They would then continue on the main trail through Burnt River Canyon, up over the Blue Mountains, and down to the Columbia River following the Umatilla River. Whitman's mission, first called Waiilatpu (Walla Walla) on the river of the same name, was set up among the Cayuse tribe. Those who needed service or supplies could travel the extra twenty-five miles east to the mission, and Whitman welcomed all in the train. Past Fort

Martin Potucek photo

Three Island Crossing Visitor Center at Glenns Ferry.

Boise, though, it did not resemble much of a wagon train. Miles separated some of the wagons and families, as impatience and excitement grew with anticipation for the journey's end. Those who could go faster, did.

Marcus Whitman and the emigrants of 1843 began dispersing as they reached the Columbia. For the scope of this book, we will leave them at this point. One interesting note: none of the members of this emigration would make it to the Willamette Valley totally overland. All would, in some form, have to float at least part of the Columbia River to reach their goal. The Barlow Road, which skirted the southern flanks of Mt. Hood and offered a continuous wagon trail, wouldn't exist for another three years.

If You Want to Go

(This description follows the trail east to west.)

Start at Border Junction, Wyoming, on U.S. Highway 30. The old route follows the highway just north. Go west into Idaho where you'll skirt around the south buttress of Big Hill. You're in the Bear River Valley, following Bear River as it turns north. The old trail passes through the east side of Montpelier. There's a historic district in town and a yearly pageant commemorating the Oregon Trai'lRendezvous. Theres' also an Oregon-California Trail Interpretive Center right on the highway you won't want to miss.

Follow Route 30 through the hamlet of Georgetown, and on to the town of Soda Springs. The highway in this section closely follows the old trail. The town takes its name from the geothermal activity there: springs and geysers spout and spit from pots, craters, and cones. These were a marvel to the emigrants, as were Steamboat Springs just down river. Those were named for regular thumping they emitted; now, they are under the waters of Alexander Reservoir just west of town near the golf course. The river makes a sharp bend south around Soda Point (aka Sheep Rock); this is where the 1843 trail headed north and then northwest toward Chesterfield.

Detour:

You can get there by following a paved road north (right) off Highway 30 from Lund (or go right on Old U.S. 30 to Bancroft). But to follow the trail northwest from Chesterfield and by the Portneuf Reservoir, where you bypass the interstate to Pocatello, you have to obtain permission from the Sho-Ban agency. That detour through the Fort Hall Reservation can be confusing and is suggested only for those who've planned ahead.

Resume the main tour by following Highway 30 over Fish Creek summit (near the head of Hudspeth's Cutoff) to the town of Lava Hot Springs, where we join the Portneuf River. Lava is a great spot to spend the night or just soak in the state-run pools. There's also historic displays, artifacts, and records at the museum in the center of town.

At the town of McCammon, go north on I-15: this will

Wayne Cornell photo

Wagon wheels wore deep ruts into the sandstone on Sinker Butte on the Oregon Trail "Dry Route," near Murphy, Idaho.

take you to Pocatello, and at the north end of town, to I-86 west. But first, in Pocatello check out the Fort Hall replica that's open to the public. It's found by taking Exit 67 from the south edge of town. Signs lead to the replica museum. The site of the real Fort Hall is actually north of town; look for the town of Fort Hall and Indian agency headquarters, where permission to visit the site is needed.

Proceeding west on I-86 you see the American Falls Reservoir (a dammed up section of the Snake River) just north of the interstate. That's where the old trail went, right along the south side of the river. Fifteen minutes past the town of American Falls is Massacre Rocks State Park. It's a fascinating place to learn about a tragedy that occurred on the trail in 1862. From there, you can follow Register Road to the Register Rock site with an equally

Wayne Cornell photo

Pioneers had to hitch several teams of oxen to each wagon to get up Sinker Creek Grade on the Oregon Trail South Alternate.

fascinating part of the Oregon Trail story, dating from 1849.

Just west is where the emigrants crossed the Raft River (take Exit 15). Now, it's not more than an irrigation ditch, but it's a significant point for folks on the trail; it's where those bound for California could split south through City of Rocks.

Detour:

Go south on 81 to Malta, then west and south on 77 through Elba and Almo. This route will loop you back north through Oakley where you can reconnect at Burley with I-84 or follow 30 west (which more closely parallels the old trail). This detour through City of Rocks is worth a day's exploration in itself. From rock climbing to old trail interpretive sites, it's chock full of adventure. Note that I-86 turns to I-84 as I-84 joins it from the south.

Wayne Cornell photo

Ward Massacre site, south of Middleton, Idaho.

As the Snake makes a bend to the north, the wagon train entered a friendlier environment.

Detour:

To follow the old trail more closely, take Exit 208 to Burley and proceed west on U.S. 30, which then, at Kimberly, runs into Idaho 50. The old trail runs right through here. Follow 30 past Hagerman, where you can jump back on I-84, or go a little farther north to join it at Bliss. This area, with Thousand Springs, fossil beds, and Malad Gorge, can take more than a day to explore.

Twin Falls was named by the large basalt outcropping that split the torrent in two, dropping 120 feet. But the real significance for the early Oregon Trail pioneer was the crossing of Rock Creek, which is a rocky gorge, like that of the Snake that it dumps into.

Detour:

Take Exit 182 and follow Highway 50 to 3800 East, through Hansen, to Rock Creek Station, an Idaho State Historical site and museum. Dating back to 1864, this was

Wayne Cornell photo

Boise River crossing at Canyon Hill, Caldwell, Idaho. The wagons had to be lowered down through the narrow notch in the rimrock, visible on the far side of the river. It was necessary to cross at this point because the flat land up and downstream was marshy and wouldn't support the heavy wagons.

the junction of the Kelton Road and the Oregon Trail. The Kelton Road came through City of Rocks, crossed the Snake just north of Buhl, and generally followed a more northerly route than the main Oregon Trail on the north side of the Snake.

At Glenns Ferry, take Exit 120 off I-84. This brings you to Three Island Crossing State Park and interpretive center, complete with self-guided trails to sites along the old trail. The first and most hazardous crossing of the Snake for most of the emigrants, this obstacle is among the best recorded along the entire route. Loops for hiking and biking are suitable for the whole family. Camping is also available, and a winery with restaurant is nearby.

From this point on to the Oregon line the old route heads in a beeline to Boise, hugging the piedmont to the north as the Snake sweeps in a big arc to the southwest. The easy way from here is to follow I-84 west to Mountain Home and on to Boise.

Detour:

If you want to chase the trail more accurately, and maybe even pedal some of this interesting section, turn off I-84 at Exit 120. Head south into Glenns Ferry briefly, then go right (west) on Bennet Mountain Road, which then heads north. Basically, keep to the pavement and go right and around the east side of Teapot Dome, just north. Follow Hot Springs Road north another few miles to Highway 20. From here, you can go either way. Either go to Mountain Home left or to more closely follow the trail, go right a few miles and turn off left (west) on Immigrant Road. This will lead you to Canyon Creek Road, which leads into Foothill Road; these two are improved county roads, but are still dirt and rock. Foothill Road hugs the foothills as it winds northwest through the old site of Mayfield. Continue to Blacks Creek Road, where after a few miles signs will direct you right to Bonneville Point where a sheltered monument and historical site are located.

Otherwise, to resume your driving route west, follow Black's Creek Road south and west a couple miles out to I-84 and head west to Boise. In Boise take Exit 57 right, west on Highway 21 almost three miles to the new Oregon Trail Historic Preserve on the right before the bridge over the Boise River. Here interpretive signs, with hiking and biking trails along the old trail including the Kelton Ramp are open to the public.

From here, to approximate the 1843 route, jump back onto I-84 west. Take Exit 54, Broadway, and follow Highways 20/26. This route follows the south side of the Boise River; the old trail runs just north between the river and this route. About twenty-five miles west of Boise go right (north) on Middleton Road to the site of the Ward Massacre site park and memorial, which is on the old trail. Resume westward on Highway 20/26 through Caldwell entering I-84 from Franklin Road and exiting at Exit 26. Follow 20/26 west through Notus and Parma. In Parma, look for signs to the Fort Boise replica. To view the site of the old fort, go a few miles north of town on Highway 20, then turn left (west) on Old Fort Boise Road. In two miles, you'll come to the wildlife management area named after the old fort. Right off the lush riverbank you'll find a monument dedicated to the fort. This is public access, and it's a great place to hike around. Before the pioneers ever came, this was an ancient seasonal gathering place.

South Alternate (Dry Route)

Much of the land along the Oregon Trail Southern Alternate hasn't changed significantly since emigrant trains used it. To follow the route, exit Interstate 84 at Hammet, west of Glenns Ferry, and take State Highway 78. The paved road follows the north bank of the Snake

Martin Potucek photo
Old Fort Boise site at junction of Boise and Snake rivers near Parma, Idaho.

Fort Boise as it looked when the first emigrant trains arrived. Floodwaters later washed away all signs of the early outpost.

River for several miles before crossing to the south bank near Bruneau Sand Dunes State Park.

The Bruneau Sand Dunes are unique in the Western Hemisphere because they are in the middle of a basin instead of on the perimeter. The highest dune is 470 feet. It is doubtful the pioneers took time off from their trek to visit the mountains of sand, but modern travelers will find the dunes well worth a stop.

Continue on Highway 78 through the towns of Bruneau and Grand View. West of Grand View, the highway crosses Castle Creek. On your left (north) can be seen an unusual bluff that resembles medieval ramparts—Castle Butte. On September 9, 1860, Indians attacked a train of forty-four emigrants led by Elijah Utter. A number of the travelers were killed, the wagons destroyed and the survivors fled west downriver. There is no marker at the site. There is a marker at Murphy, Idaho, farther west. The marker incorrectly identifies the massacre site as Sinker Creek.

Continue on Highway 78 to Marsing, Idaho. Turn left on Highway 55. At Highway 55-95 junction west of Marsing continue straight ahead to Homedale on Highway 95. In Homedale, turn left and take Highway 19, which becomes Oregon Highway 201, following the river through Adrian to Nyssa, Oregon, slightly downstream (north) of the site of Old fort Boise. Between Adrian and Nyssa Highway 201 crosses the Malheur River. It was here that soldiers found survivors of the Utter massacre who had resorted to canabalism to stay alive.

Chapter Four

George Wright and the United Tribes

On September 1, 1858, a military expedition headed by Colonel George Wright of the U.S. Army engaged and defeated a much larger force of Indians to the southwest of what is now Spokane, Washington. Wright's detachment had set out from Fort Walla Walla in the Oregon Territory almost a month earlier. Their mission was to subdue the Indian force that defeated Colonel Steptoe's military expedition earlier that spring near what is now Rosalia, Washington. Steptoe's defeat was a major military embarrassment, and government leaders felt it must be avenged.

The Spokanes, Coeur d'Alenes, and Palouses were the principle tribes that united to defend their ancestral homelands against encroachment by whites, but members of the Yakima and Pend Oreille tribes also joined their force. Polatkin, Kamaikin, Spokane Gary, and Saltese were leaders. The united Indian contingent numbered more than a thousand warriors. Mostly, the warriors' weapons were muskets, with a range of perhaps 100 yards at best, bows and arrows, lances, clubs, and axes. The Indians were also adept at using fire as a weapon (setting fire to the dry grasses before the approaching soldiers).

The battle of Four Lakes ended before sunset on September 1, 1858, when Wright's men could no longer pursue the fleeing Indians. The united tribes made their stand at a place about ten miles southwest of present day Spokane where four small natural lakes are clustered amid the basalt bedrock, prairie, and pines. After being surprised by the power and range of the new rifles used by the troops, supported by artillery fire and flanking cavalry, the native force fell back into retreat. Because Wright's force had marched 200 miles with little rest to arrive in the Spokane country, his men and horses were exhausted by battle end, and could not force a rout.

While the government forces did not sustain a single casualty, estimates of Indian casualties at Four Lakes were between twenty-five to forty killed and perhaps double that wounded. Wright used the next three days to rest his men and horses at the foot of a large hill just north of Silver Lake, the largest of the four lakes. On September 5, the troops headed northeast towards the Spokane River, starting out along the eastern shore of Silver Lake.

Leaving camp at dawn, and after five miles march, they started noticing increasing numbers of warriors. Following the army column on the flanks, with increasing acts of defiance and insults, the Indian forces seemed ready to attack. Grass fires blocking its advance brought the column to a halt. The natives made concentrated attack on the pack train (400 mules fully loaded with supplies and ammo), but Lieutenants Dandy and Gibson, in charge of the supplies, moved the train quickly onto a rocky spot where the grass grew thinly. After the soldiers lit their own fires to backburn grass immediately around them, a quick charge brought the forward part of the column through the flames and drove the attackers back. The howitzers were brought into position and fired, scattering the main body of warriors.

During a fourteen-mile running battle, all the while heading toward the Spokane River, Wright's well disciplined units continually flushed the natives from ravines, woods, and any place that afforded them shelter to regroup and counterattack. Artillery barrages were used whenever the natives gathered in large enough groups to present a clear target. The battle line extended for over a mile at times; Captain Keyes, Wright's cavalry commander, always kept a company in reserve while charging the enemy with alternating companies, keeping the conflict moving. Kamaikin, perhaps the strongest war chief and leader amongst the retreating Indians, was badly wounded by a falling tree from an overhead artillery burst. Two other chiefs of the Spokane were killed in the melee, and so the Indians' leadership was greatly reduced.

Reaching the Spokane River and following it downstream for about a mile, Wright's force pitched camp on the south bank of the river at what later came to be Fort George Wright in Spokane. The united tribes were now clusters of small groups scattered about the Spokane Valley. No more coordinated attacks were made upon Wright's group. A tense period of watching and waiting followed as the soldiers rested the next day, September 6, by the river.

On September 7, after traveling upstream about seven miles, the detachment camped for the night about two miles above the falls. Lieutenant (later Captain) John Mullan was sent out with a party of Nez Perce scouts to find a place to cross the river. Mullan was along to scout and survey an east-west road through the Rockies, and was made chief engineer of the expedition.

With the help of some Indians from the other side of the Spokane River, Mullan was shown a good ford about a mile upstream from the camp. The Indians, after this show of good will, asked for a conference with Colonel Wright. Spokane Gary crossed the river and met with Wright, explaining that he did not want to fight, but would have been killed had he not cooperated with the others. Gary had previously been quite helpful to the whites; he had been schooled in Winnipeg and converted to Christianity, and upon his return, he proceeded to convert and educate others of his tribe.

Wright's response was that, unless they wanted to be annihilated, the members of the united tribes must come before him, together with their families, arms, and worldly possessions and trust in his mercy and justice. The demand for unconditional surrender was sent to Big Star, Moses, Skloom, and Kamiakin.

Ten Indians came into camp later that day. Owhi, the old chief of the Yakimas, also came in, and was immediately put in chains. The others were let go, except for Polatkin and another who was a suspect in the murder of some Colville miners in May. Owhi was particularly important to Wright because he had been a leader in defying white settlement.

On September 8, Wright resumed his course, following the Spokane River upstream. Polatkin and Owhi were placed in chains and were forced to march for all to see. Two of Polatkin's sons challenged the troops from across the river to release their father; shots were exchanged. They were wounded and fled.

The next day, September 9, Wright's force moved eastward through the Spokane Valley. Seeing a dust cloud in the eastern distance, Wright sent three companies of dra-

Martin Potucek photo

The Cataldo Mission is Idaho's oldest building.

goons to investigate. A few miles later the advanced troops caught up with a large herd of Indian ponies being driven off into the hills mostly by women and children. There was little resistance by the Indians as the cavalry rounded up and brought back the herd.

A corral was quickly built close to the Spokane River about sixteen miles upstream from the falls (downtown Spokane today). After selecting over 100 of the best horses, over the next couple of days, Wright had a detail of men shoot the remainder of the horses. A monument stands there today by the Washington-Idaho border. This was later called Horse Slaughter Camp. Upon finding a herd of Indian cattle and several lodges filled with grain, Wright ordered his soldiers to burn the grain and capture the cattle. The grain was easy, but the cattle were wilder and more cantankerous, and all the troops could manage to do was scatter them into the foothills. Wright did not attempt

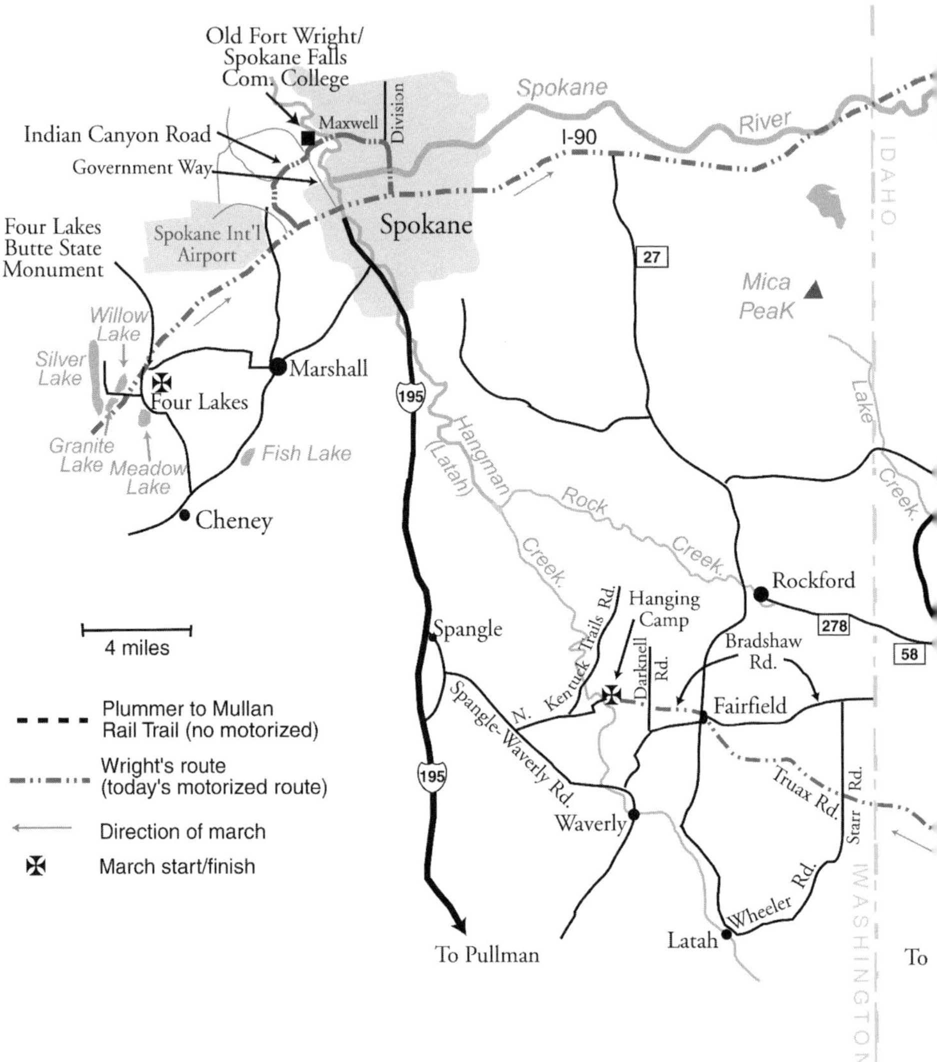
Old Fort Wright/
Spokane Falls
Com. College
Indian Canyon Road
Government Way
Maxwell
Division
Spokane
River
I-90
Spokane
Four Lakes
Butte State
Monument
Spokane Int'l
Airport
27
IDAHO
Mica
PeaK
Willow
Lake
Silver
Lake
Four Lakes
Marshall
195
Lake
Creek
Granite
Lake
Meadow
Lake
Fish Lake
Hangman
(Latah)
Rock
Creek
Cheney
Creek
Rockford
Hanging
Camp
Kentuck Trails Rd.
278
58
Spangle
Darknell
Rd.
Bradshaw
Rd.
4 miles
N.
Spangle-Waverly Rd.
Fairfield
Plummer to Mullan
Rail Trail (no motorized)
Wright's route
(today's motorized route)
195
Truax Rd.
Starr Rd.
Waverly
Direction of march
March start/finish
Wheeler Rd.
Latah
To Pullman
To
WASHINGTON

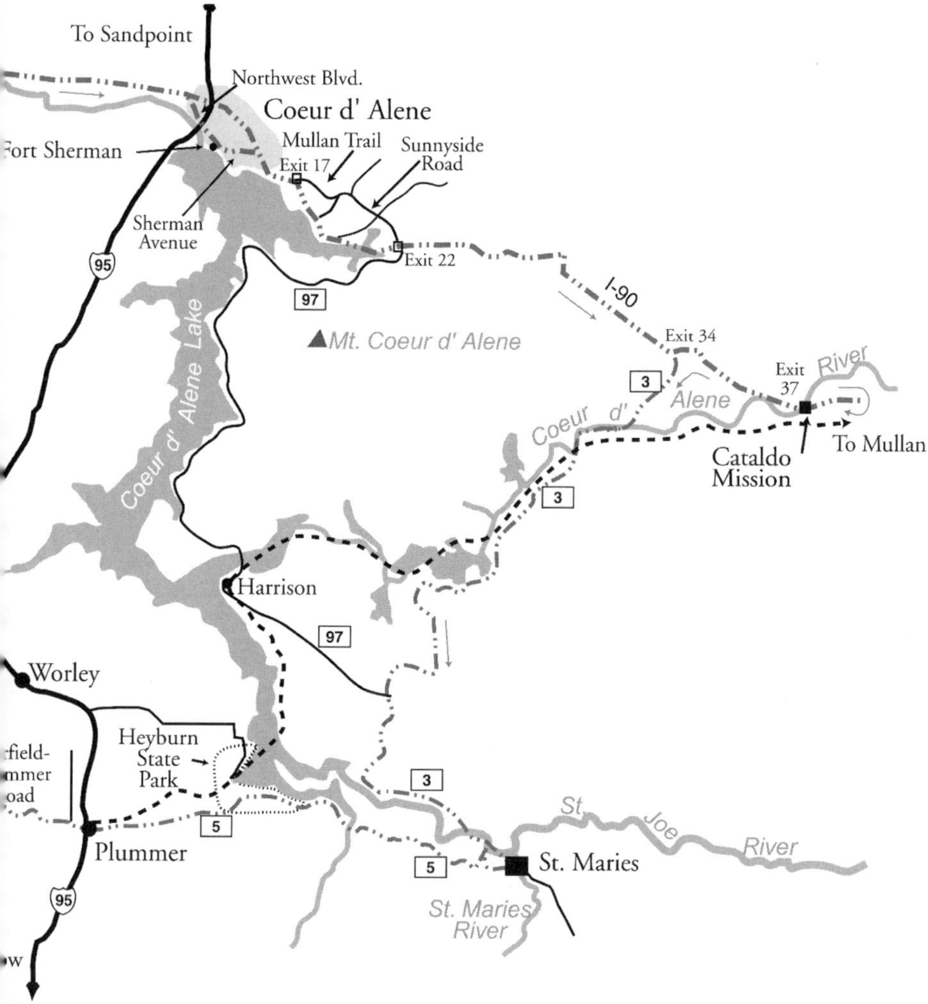
To Sandpoint
Northwest Blvd.
Coeur d' Alene
Mullan Trail
Sunnyside Road
Fort Sherman
Exit 17
Sherman Avenue
Exit 22
95
97
I-90
Mt. Coeur d' Alene
Coeur d' Alene Lake
Exit 34
Exit 37
River
3
Coeur d' Alene
To Mullan
Cataldo Mission
3
Harrison
97
Worley
Heyburn State Park
3
St. Joe River
5
Plummer
5
St. Maries
St. Maries River
95

Martin Potucek photo
Cataldo Mission interior.

to make any distinction between those who fought him and those native people who busied themselves with the agrarian tasks of farming and ranching. Some natives witnessed the slaughter of the ponies from afar, and word quickly spread about this ruthless conqueror.

Wright put out word that, if all the warriors who had fought against him did not surrender, he would annihilate all of their people. He let it be known that he was heading to Father Joset's mission where he would hold council with the Coeur d'Alene tribe. He headed his force to the Catholic mission on the Coeur d'Alene River where Joset and Chief Vincent (of the Coeur d'Alenes) lived east in the mountains.

On September 10, Father Joset sent a dispatch to Wright that the Indians "were down and suing for peace."

On September 11 the troops forded the river to the north side at the Washington–Idaho border, then marched fourteen miles east. At the northwest corner of Coeur d'Alene Lake among some large pines they camped for the night. This site would later become Fort Sherman. Today, the old site sits on the North Idaho College campus. More food caches and animals of the local Indians were found and destroyed. Continuing his negative public relations campaign, Wright painted the militants and those who were peaceful farmers and non-militants with the same brush.

Wright marched two days (September 12-13) east into the mountains to reach the Cataldo Mission, now Idaho's oldest standing building. Wright's force was vulnerable to attack as they hacked a narrow trail through thick timber and brush much of the way. The last twenty miles, through Fourth of July Canyon in the Coeur d'Alene Mountains, was slow and difficult. The howitzers were left behind, as were Mullan's wagons. A plan was hatched by some of the scattered warriors to attack the strung out column, but it never unfolded. That lack of action was a huge bit of luck for Wright for his force was at its most vulnerable point, spread out single file, sometimes over a mile, on a thin trail in dense woods.

Word had spread about where Wright was heading and that a council was to take place at the mission. Joset had lived with the Coeur d'Alenes for years, spoke their tongue, and was well-respected. Many of the participants in the two previous battles wanted forgiveness and to return to their normal lives. Joset had worked to deter their resistance against the army for he knew of the wrath and power that could be brought to bear upon them. Most of the local chiefs knew this and trusted him.

Wright arrived at the mission late on September 13. His exhausted troops rested for the next three days, also allowing word to spread of the coming council. Some say a comet even appeared, which didn't hurt Wright's credibility with the Coeur d'Alenes.

Wright was very lenient with the Coeur d'Alenes at the council that began on September 17. Many things could have contributed to this, including gratitude Wright felt for the efforts Joset made to deter the Indians' resistance against him and Steptoe. There also were reports the Coeur d'Alenes had helped Steptoe to escape. Whatever his motives, Wright dealt very lightly with the Coeur d'Alenes in contrast to the Spokanes and Palouses.

Through a stern and solemn ceremony, Wright admonished those who had fought against him. He demanded five important tribal leaders and their families travel with him back to Walla Walla and remain with him for up to a year; they would learn modern (white) ways, which he hoped would guide the rest of the tribe in the future. He also demanded the surrender of the instigators of the battle, together with all arms. He swore vengeance on any who did not come in. Polaktin was released as a gesture. A preliminary treaty was signed with the Coeur d'Alenes, headed by Chief Vincent.

On September 18 Wright marched with his prisoners and hostages thirteen miles down the north side of the Coeur d'Alene River, heading back west. The nineteenth was mostly spent ferrying supplies and the entourage across the river using their own foldable boats and Indian canoes.

The expedition moved south to the St. Joseph River, which it crossed on September 20-21, near the southern tip of Coeur d'Alene Lake by present St. Maries. The march continued around the lake westward another five miles before camp was made. A few Palouse leaders came in that afternoon, saying they were Coeur d'Alenes, trying to determine Wright's intentions.

On September 22, Wright moved eighteen miles west to a camp on Latah Creek just east of present-day Spangle, Washington. There is a monument there today that still indicates a difference of opinion about the significance of what happened there. This place is called Hanging Camp. It is much as it was; tall pines provide clusters of shade. The west side of the creek rises quickly as a basalt cliff while the east side, where the camp was pitched, sits in an open meadow.

On September 23, Wright held a council with the Spokanes at Hanging Camp. He gave the Spokanes the same terms as the Coeur d'Alenes. Chiefs Garry, Melkapsi, and Polatkin came. Wright scolded Melkapsi for his earlier insolence (he had earlier written a defiant letter to General Clarke, Wright's commander). He allowed Melkapsi to sign the treaty, along with the representatives of some other small tribes who had participated in the fights west of Spokane. By signing, the chiefs were, in effect, sheltering their bands under an umbrella of peace that Wright was now offering.

Wright's plan was to persuade Kamiakin, the only leader of the uprising who had not come in, to surrender himself, and thereby be done with the rebellious Indian leadership. Kamiakin was Owhi's brother-in-law and war chief of the Yakimas. The two had spent the previous ten years fomented resistance against white settlement. Owhi's refusal to retreat to a distant reservation in 1856 made him an incorrigible enemy in Wright's eyes. If he could not get Kamiakin, perhaps a smaller fish would do. He was told to call for Owhi's son, Qualchan, to surrender himself. Qualchan was not a chief, but he was well known throughout the entire region. He was a shining warrior who took it upon himself to avenge wrongs done to the native peoples by encroaching whites. He was a valuable prize for Wright. He threatened Owhi's death if his son did not come in.

By a quirk of fate, Qualchan did not get word of

Wright's ultimatum. On September 24, Qualchan, accompanied by his beautiful wife, Whist-alks, and his brother, Lo-kout, rode into camp, unaware of the ill will waiting for him. The three were pulled down off their horses. In less than a quarter of an hour, Qualchan was hanged. Lo-kout and Whist-alks were able to remount their horses in the confusion and escape with bullets flying. Qualchan put up a fierce struggle after he realized the intentions of his captors. It was a futile effort; a half dozen men were upon him and bound him tightly. Wright never even came out to meet the warrior he had sentenced to death.

While Wright and his main force were camped on Latah Creek, Major Grier took a cavalry detachment off to the Steptoe battle site, just twelve miles south, to recover the two buried artillery pieces and gather up the remains of the dead for later burial at Fort Walla Walla. The scene described by Grier must have had a dour effect on Wright.

That same night a number of Palouses surrendered to Wright; he arrested fifteen of them immediately and hanged six shortly thereafter. The rest were put in chains. Latah Creek, on which they were camped, was now being called Hangman Creek; to the local Indians it was Nedwauld River.

On September 26, Wright headed his force back to Walla Walla, together with the prisoners, hostages, and their families. On September 30 he camped on the banks of the Palouse River, after four days march in cold and wet conditions. There, he called to council the Palouses, the last major participant in the Spokane battles. Not including them in his promised treaties to come, he hanged four warriors for crimes going back to that spring. The only noteworthy incident on the way back to Walla Walla occurred just as the group left Fort Taylor, while crossing the Tucannon River. Old chief Owhi, who had his hands

Martin Potucek photo

Hanging Camp site on Hangman Creek

bound and his feet chained to his horse, made a break for it at the river. He was shot dead after a short chase. He must have known it was hopeless, but he was the father of his son, Qualchan.

Varying accounts credit Wright with hanging up to twenty-seven men from the united tribes since the battles, while not one Coeur d'Alene was executed. It's obvious that Wright was much more severe with the Palouse and Spokane than with the Coeur d'Alene; their past peace with the whites had been unbroken until recently.

Significance

Intending that this would be the last battle between red and white, Wright maximized the effect of his avenge-and-conqueror strategy. He stated he would sign no peace treaty with the Indians at that time, but would wait a year, and if they had abided by his dictates, then he would formalize the peace, which he never did.

Colonel George Wright did succeed in his task. Never again would any of the northern tribes of the region rise against the government and white culture. After that, the

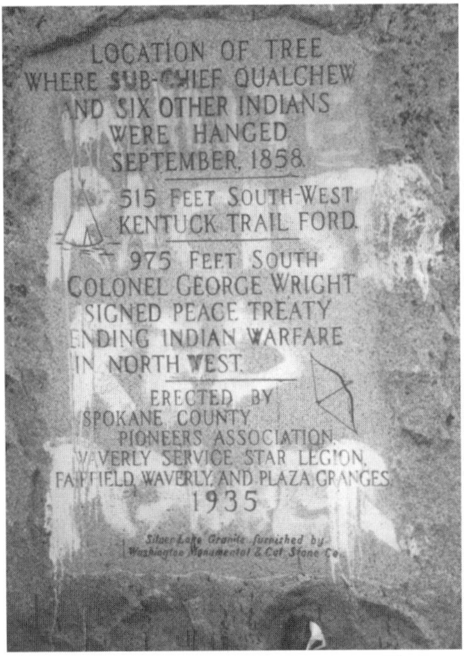

Martin Potucek photo

Vandalized marker at Hanging Camp site is evidence of lingering unrest.

floodgates of white settlement and the search for gold would change the face of their ancestral lands. Where fishing, hunting, gathering, and moving their camps to follow the seasons, would be displaced by tilling the soil, clearing the forests, and raising stock.

Wright went on to become a general and fight Indians in both Oregon and California. In a bizarre twist of fate, he and his wife drowned off the California-Oregon coast in the summer of 1865. He was traveling north on an overburdened steamer in a fierce storm when they hit a point called Dragon Rocks.

If You Want to Go

To begin following Wright's campaign route, start at the small town of Four Lakes, Washington. It's about eight miles southwest of downtown Spokane. Take I-90 west out of Spokane, and take Exit 270 to 904. Just off the freeway and before Four Lakes, take a left on Melville Road. Just a bit down Melville will take you to a marker on the right (south) side of the road. If you want to find Silver Lake, where Wright camped, follow 904 to Four Lakes to Granite Lake Road at the north end of town. Follow it less than a mile to Taylor Road, which goes right and leads you under the freeway to Silver Lake Road, which goes left. This road winds around and between Willow Lake and Granite Lake and leads you directly to the eastern shore of Silver Lake, the route Wright took on September 5, 1858.

The Indians retreated northwest from here. Spokane Plains Battlefield Park can be found directly north six miles at the intersection of U.S. 2 and South Dover Road. But to continue along Wright's general way, get back on I-90 heading east. Take Exit 277B to Spokane International Airport and go right on Geiger Rd. Go left where Geiger meets Sunset Boulevard and then a quick right onto Deska. At the intersection of Assembly Road go left, which turns into Indian Canyon Road. Just past the golf course about a half mile, as you head down into the winding canyon road, there's a trail off to the left. This is where Chief Spokane Gary lived and died; there's a marker erected for him there. He's buried in the Greenwood Cemetery just down the hill.

Go left at the bottom of the canyon at Government Way. Proceed about a mile and a half to Fort George Wright Drive; this takes you by the old fort grounds (now Mukogawa Fort Wright Institute) and Spokane Falls Community College on the left. Wright's campsite was to the left (west) before you cross over the Meenach Bridge. A part of the Centennial Trail pathway and trails off of it will take you right to the river's edge.

Crossing the bridge you can go right up Pettet Drive, which winds south and then east into Maxwell. Turn right on Division, which leads you across the Spokane River, and to I-90 left, and heading east again.

Bike Note:

If you want to more closely follow Wright's route, hop on your bike back at the Meenach Bridge, and pedal all the way past Coeur d'Alene on the Centennial Trail, a beautiful dedicated bike and pedestrian pathway. There are sign-

posts, historical markers, numerous access points, and even potties along the way. It closely follows the river and the northern shore of Lake Coeur d'Alene, much of it very close to Wright's path.

Take Exit 299 off I-90 and pull into the Stateline rest area. The Centennial Trail comes to this point, too. Go west just a quarter mile on the trail to find the Horse Slaughter Camp monument. This was where, on September 9 and 10, 1858, the large herd of Indian ponies were killed by Wright's men. Continue east on I-90 (you're now in Idaho) to Coeur d'Alene. Take Exit 11 and then go south on Northwest Boulevard. After 1.5 miles go left on Lincoln Way and then right on River Ave.; this will lead you through the middle of the North Idaho College campus. Old Fort Sherman is right there close to the lake. Take College Drive to Lakeshore Drive to Park Drive to a right on Mullan Avenue (remember Lieutenant Mullan?). This will lead you back to Northwest Boulevard (around beautiful Blackwell City Park) where you turn right. Northwest turns into Sherman Avenue, Coeur d'Alene's downtown. At the end of Sherman Avenue. in the east end of town signs will direct you back onto I-90 heading east.

Note: You can also take the Centennial Trail at the east end of Coeur d'Alene before jumping back on the freeway. It's a beautiful paved promenade that closely follows the lakeshore for a good ten miles east. A dedicated non-motorized pathway that parallels the old highway, it's accessed via Sherman or Mullan Ave. to Coeur d'Alene Lake Drive. Historical markers, potties, and picnic facilities grace the way.

Taking I-90 east to the Cataldo Mission is the fastest way to get there, but it's not exactly the path Wright took. If you take Exit 17, the Mullan Trail Road, it will connect with Sunnyside Road, which will take you back to I-90 at

Exit 22; this will take you around Blue Creek Bay, which Wright also had to do. This is where Wright's expedition encountered a narrow Indian trail through steep, dense forest and brush. Following the Cedar Creek drainage, the road winds up to Fourth of July Summit and into Fourth of July Canyon. This was some of the most strenuous part of Wright's excursion. It was also the worst part of the building of the Mullan Road, a major undertaking a few years later led by Captain John Mullan, that would lead miners and settlers out west all the way from the Missouri River.

As the canyon opens up to the lush Coeur d'Alene River Valley, go another four miles to Exit 40. Here you'll find the old mission, Idaho's oldest structure, still standing. A state park has been built around it; it's a great place for lunch and wandering around. This is where Wright spent September 13 through 18 and convened his council with the Coeur d'Alenes on September 17. This was Wright's farthest point east.

To resume Wright's campaign trail, go back west on I-90 to Exit 34 where you'll go south on Idaho 3; this road winds through lush and rolling country as it follows the Coeur d'Alene River for the next fifteen miles. Just beyond Cave Lake, one of the many lakes that chain off of the river, Highway 3 goes south and leaves the river as it approaches the town of St. Maries. In town, bear right at the main intersection and take Idaho 5 west. This beautiful and shady section of roadway leads, in nineteen miles, to U.S. Highway 95 and the town of Plummer on the Coeur d'Alene Indian Reservation.

Bike Note:

At Plummer or Heyburn State Park (you come to the park about six miles east on Highway 5) you can pick up a new rail-trail, the Trail of the Coeur d'Alenes, that will be one of the most dramatic in the west. Starting in Plummer, cutting through a spectacular canyon that follows Plummer Creek, it leads through chain lakes and over river levees that follow the Coeur d'Alene River all the way to Mullan, Idaho. Wright didn't go that far east, but the reclaimed Union Pacific line takes you right past the old Cataldo mission on the opposite side of the river. You can access it from the town of Cataldo just east of the mission at Exit 43, if you want to ride the entire section from Cataldo to Plummer. This section, which follows closely a lot of Wright's path, consists of thirty-five miles of hard surface pathway, complete with restrooms, picnic facilities, landscaping, and interpretive signs. Most of the way you are either over water or right next to it. A 3,000 ft. long trestle over Lake Coeur d'Alene is a highlight of the trail, which boasts a raised mid section that used to swing open for boat traffic. Heyburn State Park, just south of the bridge, offers overnight camping for trail users. Also note that a nice system of bike and horse trails is open to the public at Heyburn. A number of those trails cross the original Mullan Trail which cuts right through the park.

From the town of Plummer, Wright marched due west eighteen miles to the site of Hanging Camp on Latah (Hangman Creek). To get there by today's means, take the county road west out of Plummer (starts out as A Street). Just a short way out, it turns into the Plummer-Fairfield Road as it jogs right and winds around a hill. After it crosses Plummer Creek, wind around and climb through woods as the road continues west. At about eight miles from Plummer, it turns into Truax Road. This is also the Washington state line, where the surface becomes pavement. About fifteen miles west of Plummer come to the hamlet of Fairfield. Turn left at the intersection of Main and Railroad where there's a stop sign. Pass Ye Galleon Press, cross the railroad tracks and turn right (north) onto

Highway 27. In a few blocks at the north end of town go left onto Bradshaw Road, which turns back to gravel. Proceed west a few miles and cross Hangman Creek. In less than two miles turn right on North Kentuck Trail (paved). Go less than a mile to a spot where you drop down into Hangman Creek; a historical marker will direct you to the right (north) side where you can pull in to a dirt turn-around.

You'll find a monument under some pines marking the dire events that happened here and that gave this stream its name. This is Hanging Camp, where Qualchan and others met their end. Controversy and bitter feelings are still generated from this site and the monument that marks it. The tone of the message inscribed in stone here doesn't seem to tone down the righteousness of the deeds done. Perhaps there is room for more than one message. Take a quiet moment to ponder the place as it was then; hundreds of soldiers were camped all about; water, firewood, and grass were all abundant. This is where Wright's campaign ended; he had succeeded beyond even his own expectations. The region was now safe for the growing wave of immigrants; native resistance had been utterly crushed. No matter what point of view you come from, the events that happened here were to shape the course of things to come, forever.

To return to Spokane the quickest way, just go back Kentuck Trail the way we came, but follow it west, staying on the pavement, to the Spangle-Waverly Road. Turning right there will bring you to Spangle, U.S. 195, and Spokane.

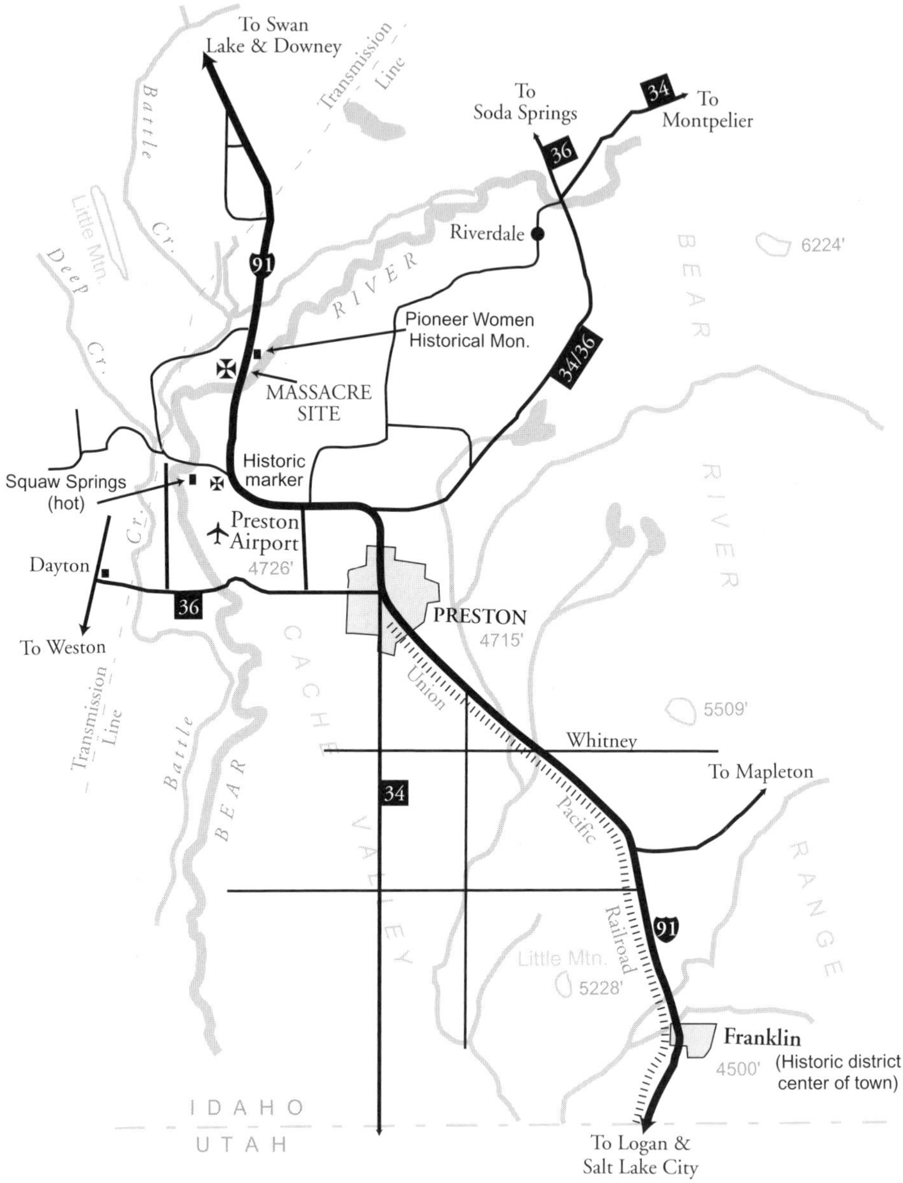
To Swan
Lake & Downey
Transmission
Line
To
Soda Springs
To
Montpelier
34
36
Battle
Cr.
Little Mtn.
Deep
Cr.
Riverdale
6224'
BEAR
RIVER
91
Pioneer Women
Historical Mon.
34/36
MASSACRE
SITE
Historic
marker
Squaw Springs
(hot)
Preston
Airport
4726'
Dayton
To Weston
PRESTON
4715'
Union
Pacific
Railroad
5509'
Whitney
To Mapleton
CACHE
VALLEY
Battle
BEAR
Transmission
Line
RANGE
Little Mtn.
5228'
Franklin
4500'
(Historic district
center of town)
IDAHO
UTAH
To Logan &
Salt Lake City

Chapter Five

Bear River Massacre

Colonel Patrick Edward Connor came from Ireland, born on St. Patrick's Day, 1820. He went to school in New York and joined the U.S. Army in 1839, serving in the cavalry. After leaving the army in 1844, he moved to Texas in 1846 where he joined the Texas Volunteers as the Mexican War broke out.

When the California gold rush started in 1849, Connor followed quickly, arriving there in January 1850. In 1853 he joined a group called the California Rangers, organized with the purpose of hunting down the bandit Joaquin Murieta. That deed done, he settled down in Stockton, California, married, and worked as a surveyor. That led to various civil posts and contracting services, including building a city waterworks and foundations for the state capitol building.

Even while a civilian, he maintained an interest in military affairs. He was a true patriot, for when the Civil War broke out in 1861, he repudiated the southern sympathizers in the local Stockton Guard he commanded. In August of that year he was mustered as colonel of the Third

California Infantry, organized to protect the overland wagon and mail route, and the new telegraph line between California and Utah.

Connor took five companies of infantry from California and arrived in the Salt Lake area in late October 1862. He established Fort Douglas, just east of Salt Lake City. A rising mutual distrust between Brigham Young, the Mormon leader, and Colonel Connor, led Connor to locate his barracks away from the center of the Mormon stronghold.

When Connor and his men arrived in the area, a tense situation between whites and the local Shoshonis and Bannocks had reached a boiling point. For a few years now, murders, robberies, and the stealing of stock had created a pattern of recurrent retribution. Acts of Indian violence against whites during that period are well documented. What is not so well documented are the acts against the Indians perpetrated by the whites. In many incidents, the Cache Valley Shoshonis acted in reprisal against incursions into their ancestral lands.

In the late fall of 1862 Chiefs Bear Hunter, Sagwitch, and Pocatello had gathered their bands into a large community on the banks of the Bear River. This was the northern end of the Cache Valley that stretched north-south between Idaho and Utah at their eastern borders. This lush, well-watered valley was used for countless generations by these indigenous people as foraging and winter camping grounds. Natural hot springs nearby also attracted them here as a winter refuge. Following that tradition, this would be the three bands' winter camp and the base for some of their more rebellious individuals' raids in their growing antagonism with the whites.

The Mormons had coexisted with the Indians using a policy of offering what they could to appease them rather than fighting them outright. The "better to feed than fight" policy worked well when stores were plentiful; as winter came on, the abundance diminished, and tensions grew.

A number of factors contributed to the Indians' dissatisfaction with their treatment by the whites. One was the huge size of the Indian agency that was established to administer them; at the time, the territorial capital was in Oregon City, hundreds of miles west with only a few agents to deal with dozens of widely scattered tribes. Another factor was that the U.S. government was involved with a much bigger conflict back east: the Civil War. Also, the Northwestern Shoshonis had the unfortunate luck of living right in the middle of one of the main westering routes, the Oregon Trail. Resources were stretched thin in this new territory, and priorities were elsewhere.

The camp, where Battle Creek joins the Bear River, lies about twelve miles northwest of the Mormon town of Franklin, the closest settlement. Franklin was originally thought to be within Utah, but when the line was finally surveyed, it was discovered that Franklin was located in Idaho Territory, making it Idaho's first town.

Connor had developed a plan to deal with the Indians first, then turn to the Mormons, who were considered by the military brass to be rebels of the U.S. government. Connor had to deal with soldiers among his ranks who were sympathetic with the South, and perhaps to the Confederacy. He had received reports that the Mormons had traded with the Indians for years, sometimes supplying them with guns and ammunition.

As a winter storm with sub-zero temperatures blew in, Connor hatched a plan. From Fort Douglas on January 23, 1863, he would move his force in two parts. He would march to the Indians' Bear River camp north of Salt Lake some 150 miles. He would press his troops in a forced march and launch a surprise attack. One part of his force would march by daylight, out in full view, where he knew word of their coming would get to the Indian camp. Another part of his force would follow behind a half day, by dark. He was fable to recruit the famed Mormon Guide, Porter Rockwell, to lead the expedition.

This first visible force would not march in an organized fashion. They would appear slovenly and undisciplined. They would camp out in obvious places for all to see, seeming vulnerable and aloof. But a crucial element of Connor's plan was to follow up this first force with a strong cavalry detachment that would travel by night, camping in hidden places, keeping as unseen as possible.

Here's a brief journal of the force's progress to Franklin:

> January 21, 1863: Connor gives order to move expedition out of Camp Douglas.
>
> January 22: First regiment of infantry, under Captain Hoyt, move out in a blinding snowstorm, traveled thirteen miles.
>
> January 23: Hoyt's infantry covers twenty-five miles in still bad weather, makes it to the Weber River.
>
> January 24: Hoyt's force makes another eighteen miles to Willard. Connor's three regiments of cavalry depart Fort Douglas, intending to travel unnoticed and by night.
>
> January 25: Hoyt marches another fourteen miles, starts losing soldiers to frostbite and exhaustion.
>
> January 26: Hoyt marches to Mendon (twenty-five miles) and lays over the next day to rest.

Martin Potucek photo

The monument is to the old ferry and bridge. The Bear River Massacre site is in the background, at right.

> January 28: Just after midnight the force departs for Franklin (thirty-four miles) and camps. The cavalry arrives ten hours before the infantry, who are frozen and exhausted.

Connor's force camped at Franklin for the night, on January 28, and a short one it would be. By 3 a.m. they had packed and resumed heading north. Captain Hoyt was supposed to have left by 1 a.m., but it took him an additional two hours to locate locals who could guide him to the exact spot of the Shoshoni encampment. After help from Mormon elders, two brothers, Edmond and Joseph Nelson, were recruited to guide Hoyt's infantry north the dozen miles to their goal.

The troops were bone tired; some had been left behind on the way due to frostbite and exhaustion. It was below zero, clear and starry on the morning of January 29, 1863;

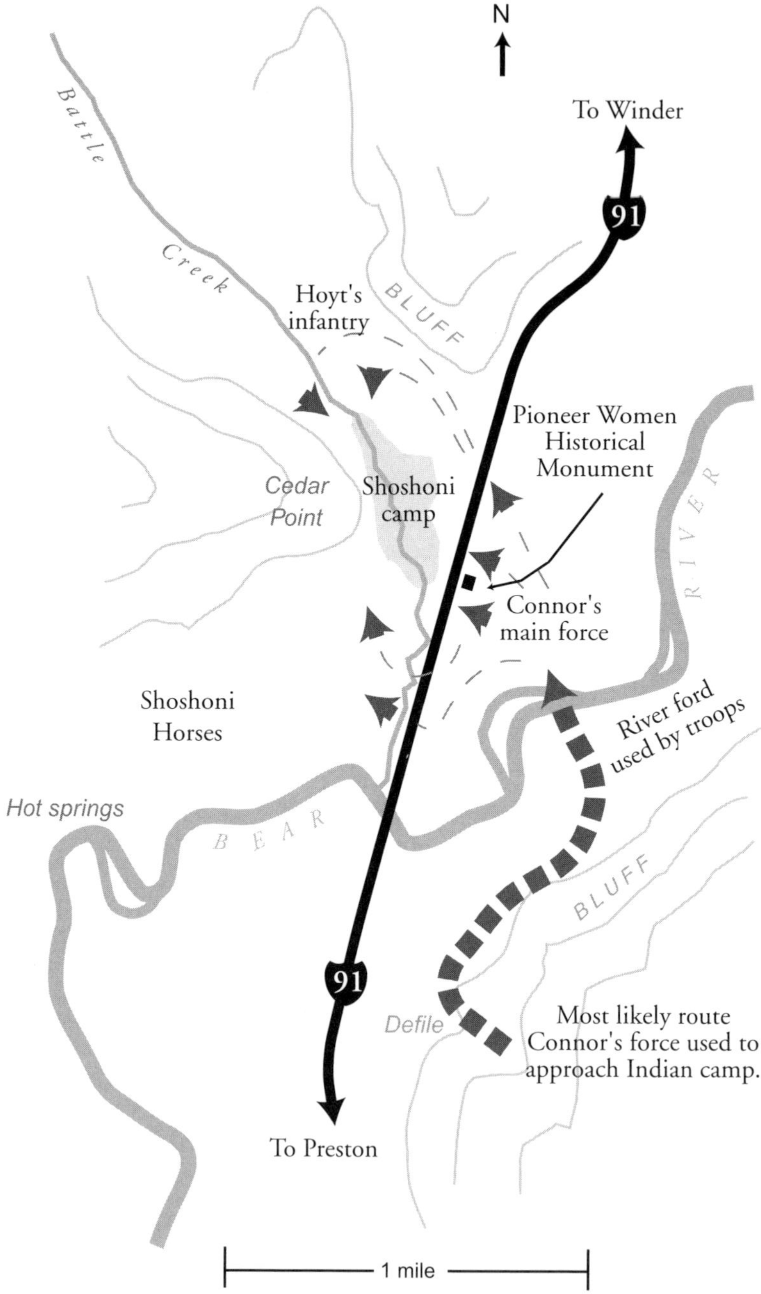
N
To Winder
91
Battle
Creek
Hoyt's infantry
BLUFF
Pioneer Women
Historical
Monument
Cedar Point
Shoshoni camp
RIVER
Connor's main force
Shoshoni Horses
River ford used by troops
Hot springs
BEAR
BLUFF
91
Defile
Most likely route
Connor's force used to
approach Indian camp.
To Preston
1 mile

Martin Potucek photo
Historical signboards and monument at massacre site.

two feet of snow lay on the ground. Two cannons had to be left behind in a snowdrift, and no one had thought sleds would be needed.

Before reaching Franklin, the cavalry caught up and passed the forward infantry. Reaching the river across from the Indian camp at dawn, Connor's cavalry found the Indians had fortified the area with rifle trenches and breastworks woven from willows. The Indians were well prepared and waiting. Some sources say the trenches were just big steps cut into the earthen banks, dug there to allow access to the higher ground. There's also conjecture that the thick marsh willows that grew abundantly around the camp and served as a natural wind break afforded the defenders their best cover from the onslaught.

There was a delay, however, because the infantry fell behind the cavalry. Major McGarry with his advance cavalry was the first to arrive at 6 a.m.—more than an hour before dawn. Connor's main cavalry force left Franklin about 4 a.m. and passed Hoyt's infantry four miles out. Only half his force was there at first light, the

Martin Potucek photo

This plaque honors Morman women who tended wounded from the Bear River fight. Another plaque on the monument commemmorates the actual battle.

planned time of attack. The defenders started to insult and jeer the soldiers. Some insult apparently was too much for the Colonel, because he abandoned caution and gave the order to charge.

The cavalry charged, crossing the sandy river bottom, sheeted in ice that broke and slid under the horses' hooves. Fourteen soldiers died in that first attempt, which was repulsed by accurate fire from the enemy. After two more attacks, Connor pulled his troops back. By now, the infantry had caught up, but Connor's haste had led to heavy losses in the early assaults.

Connor's assembled force of California volunteers and regular Army were surprised that over a dozen of their own lay dead after the first volley. Their next two attempts, while more cautious and less costly, got them nowhere.

Connor split his force into three parts: a frontal push just to get their attention, a detachment that came down from the north following the river, and another flanking movement coming up the river from the south (see battle map). It would be a good way to test his perimeter. Conner sent McGarry to cross the river via a ford the Nelson brothers had pinpointed; this greatly helped the horses cross the breakable ice that had caused many in the first attack to fall. Connor was afraid the enemy would sneak out the back door, and McGarry's move was intended to let none out of his trap.

The flanking movements worked well; they pushed the Shoshonis out of their dug-in defenses. There were thickets of willows hiding their teepees, down low where they were protected from the initial enemy fire. As the Indians were flushed out of the area where Battle Creek joins Bear River, they exposed themselves to more fire. A position of volunteers had established themselves on a bluff above the creek; hundreds died in the following minutes. After the second assault, which included the flanking movements intended to concentrate the battle, fierce hand-to-hand fighting followed for the next two hours. Soldiers armed with revolvers had a huge advantage in the close quarters struggle. Some even had two side arms, which worked with even deadlier effectiveness.

After only a few hours between 250 and 350 Indians, almost the entire camp, lay dead, making it the worst loss of Indian life in a single battle in American history. Some said that bodies were lying in piles; warriors, women, children, and old ones all; none were excepted.

Local observers after the melee reported looting by some of the soldiers and atrocities committed against the dead, dying, and women. It's understandable that emotions were high after the action, and Connor did make an effort to rein in his men. One San Francisco reporter did accompany the force and witness the scene firsthand. The commander did not want to be known as a squaw killer, but various reports convey that what happened after was not something to be proud of.

On the other side, fourteen soldiers were killed, and forty-nine wounded. Many more lost toes and feet to frostbite. Reports say up to two dozen Indians escaped, including Chief Sagwitch and his son. Reports disagree about the number of women and children taken captive. Connor himself reported that 160 were taken. Local eye witnesses say the number was very small, perhaps a handful. This second opinion may be more accurate considering the ferocity with which the women were reported to have fought.

Wounded soldiers were hauled on wagons to Franklin for care. Other settlements also took in the wounded. The Mormons were much friendlier and more helpful to his troops after the battle. Some speculate that expected Indian reprisal against them, if Connor's force failed, contributed to this.

Significance

Aside from this overall calming effect on the region, until the end of 1866, close to 400 more Indians were reported killed in twenty-seven military actions against them. In late September, 1864, a standoff occurred between a large band of Shoshonis, perhaps 300, and the inhabitants of Franklin. It ended with no loss of life, but it represents the tension between whites and natives after the massacre.

If You Want to Go

Although Connor's expedition started out from Camp Douglas (at the present University of Utah site), the route

Martin Potucek photo

Franklin, Idaho, was the first white community established in Idaho. The Mormon founders thought it was in Utah. The attackers passed just south of Franklin on the to attack the Bear River camp.

description following will be limited to the distance between Franklin and the site of the massacre. Also included is a brief synopsis of Connor's progress to get to the town of Franklin from Camp Douglas.

From the central historic district of the town of Franklin, proceed north on U.S. Highway 91 about seven miles to the town of Preston. Just north of town, where Highway 34 splits off right (east), stay left on 91, heading west.

At 1.5 miles from that intersection, 91 starts a big sweeping right hand curve as it turns north. Towards the end of this curve is a state historical marker on the right (east) side of the road. It's titled Bear River Battle.

Proceed another mile and a half and pull over at a small

parking area on the right. At this site is a stone monument and plaque that mark the one-sided battle or massacre. Interestingly, the front of the monument commemorates Mormon pioneer women who ministered to the wounded soldiers after the battle. Only on the side of the monument (not facing the highway) is the plaque to the massacre itself. Off to the side by the state historical signs are native American tokens (tripods with eagle feathers, beads, and notes) of the massacre. In 1990 the site was declared a National Historic Landmark by the National Park Service. There is currently an effort under way to make it a National Historic Site; that would require, by current standards, more than a quarter section of land to be purchased, involving millions of dollars in federal funds. Right now, the area is owned by a few local white families; abandoned houses and farm implements remind one of an agrarian past, not of more ancient times.

From the monument site looking due west, you can see Cedar Point, which rises 200 vertical feet, where sharpshooters picked off Shoshone as they fled the cover of the willows below. Just a few dozen yards north on Highway 91 you can follow Hot Springs Road left, off the highway, around the base of Cedar Point, to Wayland Hot Springs. This was where the Shoshone for generations soaked in the healing waters. And you can look across back toward the monument, over the bottom land where the horse herd grazed.

Descriptions from local past and present say that Battle Creek now flows into Bear River at a different point than 140 years ago. But, aside from the highway and farms, the place probably looks pretty much now as it did then. Today, it is pasture and meadow, and has never been set aside for protection from souvenir hunters. The bones of many still lie here, and to some, it is sacred land.

Events Pertinent to the Bear River Massacre

April 7, 1862: Dept. of the Pacific (U.S. Army) general order: "hang on the spot". . . "every Indian captured". . . "engaged in hostilities against whites". . . "women and children in all cases being spared."

January 14, 1863: G. Clayton and H. Bean were murdered by an unknown band of Indians in the Cache Valley.

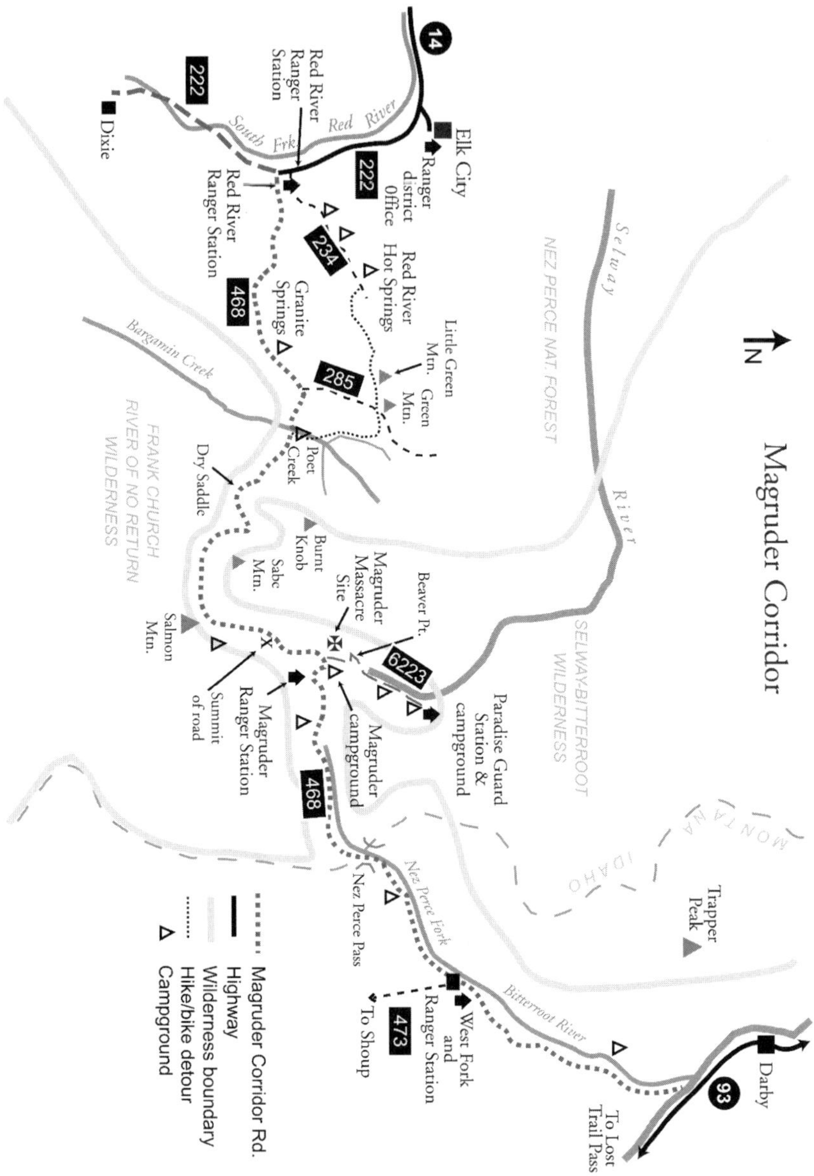
Magruder Corridor
N
14
Elk City
Ranger district Office
222
Red River Ranger Station
South Frk. Red River
Red River Ranger Station
Dixie
234
Red River Hot Springs
468
Granite Springs
Little Green Mtn.
Green Mtn.
285
Bargamin Creek
Poet Creek
Dry Saddle
Burnt Knob
Sabe Mtn.
Magruder Massacre Site
Beaver Pt.
6223
Salmon Mtn.
Summit of road
Magruder Ranger Station
Magruder campground
Paradise Guard Station & campground
NEZ PERCE NAT. FOREST
Selway River
SELWAY-BITTERROOT WILDERNESS
FRANK CHURCH RIVER OF NO RETURN WILDERNESS
468
Nez Perce Pass
Nez Perce Fork
West Fork and Ranger Station
473
To Shoup
Bitterroot River
Darby
93
To Lost Trail Pass
Trapper Peak
MONTANA
IDAHO
Magruder Corridor Rd.
Highway
Wilderness boundary
Hike/bike detour
Campground

Chapter Six

The Magruder Corridor

January 1863

In the late summer of 1863 Idaho had just become a territory unto itself. Splitting off from Washington state, it first included what's now Montana and Wyoming. Previously, it was part of Washington Territory, which then stretched from the Missouri River to the Pacific Ocean. What allowed Idaho its autonomy was a wave of white humanity that washed over it in roughly the years of the American Civil War, the early 1860s. That flood was triggered by E. D. Pierce's discovery of gold in the mountains above the Clearwater River in 1860, in a place they called Canal Gulch.

Within a year of that first sign of "color" (visible gold in the placers) in the region, miners had turned to prospecting the mountains and waters to the south and east. Strikes occurred in places like Elk City, Florence, and Warrens. Within a few weeks, a town would spring up; hundreds, even thousands would pour into a wide spot in the wilderness. Nobody seemed to mind that most of the stampeding for the precious metal was on Nez Perce treaty land, or that it was restricted to white incursion. Where

Hill Beachy tracked the killers of Lloyd Magruder to San Francisco.

gold had been discovered, people followed, ignoring any government rules.

The town of Lewiston sprang up, seemingly overnight, to supply the miners. It was first called Ragtown, due to the proliferation of tents and their canvas tatters created by the sun and wind. Lewiston became the launch point overland for the gold fields. Steamboats by 1860 could safely make it up the Columbia and Snake Rivers all the way from Portland. Lewiston was neatly situated at the headwaters (the highest point navigable by boat) on the Snake River. It lay just downstream from where the Clearwater flowed into the Snake. For most, it was just a couple of days ride over rugged trail to Pierce and Oro Fino, where the Idaho gold rush started.

As new gold strikes opened up new areas for exploitation, Lewiston became more established as a distribution point for goods both north, south, and even across the mountains into the buffalo country of western Montana. One enterprising newcomer was Lloyd Magruder, who quickly saw that all this rush for gold would require someone to supply the miners and prospectors.

Magruder had established himself as a respected merchant, supplying folks in Lewiston and outlying areas, using mule pack strings for transport. He had learned the needed skills while serving as a young officer in the Army.

Martin Potucek photo

Western end of Magruder Corridor (FR 468).

He came to Lewiston from Marysville, California, where he ran a newspaper. He had recently moved his wife and family up to the new territorial capital, which by 1863, still didn't have a school.

Hill Beachy was a good friend of the Magruders. Beachy had built one of the first permanent structures in town, the Luna House. It was a shallow-roofed, hewn log structure that served as hotel, restaurant, and watering hole for the town's business community. In 1863 it was still the only two-story building around. Magruder and Beachy had become friends, even though the more somber Beachy was less trusting by nature. They were both hard working businessmen, but Magruder needed more adventure in his life.

This trip across the mountains fulfilled Magruder's short term business goals, but he needed something more substantial, something that would put his mark on this new land and all its potential. Magruder had shown an interest in the new territorial government and was well-liked and well-known for his fair and reasonable demeanor. He didn't realize as he was preparing for his trip that his name was being bandied about town to represent the new territory back in Congress.

Thus it was that Magruder had spent most of the last week preparing a half dozen men and five dozen mules for a late summer trip over the Bitterroots to Bannack in the Beaverhead region of southwest Montana. It was not a trip to be taken lightly. It was already the middle of August and the summer heat of Lewiston was no insurance against snow in the high passes. Also, there was really no law in the new territory yet. Fort Lapwai was just a rumor at this time, and there wasn't even a sheriff. Nez Perce bands were scattered about the higher meadows this time of year, but they busied themselves mostly with hunting, fishing, and gathering roots, preparing for the coming winter. And although most newcomers were honest men, there were bad ones, too, who would prey on miners, laden with gold dust, and others passing through the mountains.

Magruder knew of the dangers; he had made trips similar to this one. Moving with a large mule string and a well armed crew, he felt secure in his plan. He would head out first for Elk City, a week's ride south through the Camas Prairie and into the mountains. There, he would restock a store he had established the year before, catering mostly to the miners. Then, after seeing to the needs of other Elk City merchants, he would resume his trek to Bannack (in western Montana) with about a dozen less mules.

The trail Magruder was following had been improved since the coming of the white miners, but it was an ancient Indian trail, what we now call the Southern Nez Perce

Martin Potucek photo
Looking south toward the Salmon River from Nez Perce Pass.

Trail. It had been used for generations by those people in their seasonal migrations over the Bitterroots. It allowed them to hunt buffalo on the high plains in summer and return before snows to their warm, low-lying winter camps on the Salmon, Clearwater, and Snake Rivers. The trail, although mostly direct, climbed higher than 8,000 feet, and it was not unusual to camp above 7,000 feet.

Interestingly, this was the route that Lewis and Clark neglected in late 1805 when searching for a trail through the Salmon River drainage. Toby, the Lemhi guide had taken Clark with a small party down the river and showed Clark how violent the water was. This is where some say the term "River of No Return" came from. This is also the trail that Samuel Parker in 1835 took west, guided by Indians, which led him over the Bitterroots when he came seeking to establish missions for the Presbyterian Church. Now it was used by packers and miners traversing the mountains between the new gold strikes of Montana and the older diggings in Idaho.

Magruder was well prepared for the trip except for the number of his trail crew, which was a bit light. At Elk City he lost a couple of regulars to gold fever, and so after resuming the trail to Bannack, he welcomed a couple of travelers heading their way. They were hired on as extra hands to help with the animals. Magruder recognized one of them, James Romain, as the plasterer at the building where he worked for the newspaper in California. What Magruder did not realize was that the two men were part of a plan to rob him of his gold on the return trip over the mountains.

Another man a few days later came upon the pack train and asked that he might join them, as it was much safer not to travel alone. This man, by the name of Lower, knew the other two newcomers, but none of them pretended to know each other. It was part of the plan to gain Magruder's confidence and get to know Magruder's agenda. Magruder didn't really need any more men, but he told Lower if he could cook, then he could eat and travel with the party. Because he carried gold now out of Elk City, Magruder took the precaution of posting a nightly two-man watch.

Once over the crest of the Bitterroots, the party made good time and arrived in Bannack. But finding it almost abandoned, Magruder heard that mostly everybody had left for the new strike at Alder Gulch, seventy-five miles east near Virginia City. He felt he had no choice but to follow the miners there; they were the market for his goods. Virginia City also had a new sheriff named Henry Plummer, who was later hanged for masterminding a series of murders and bushwhacks. It's uncertain whether Plummer was in on the plan to rob Magruder.

Martin Potucek photo

Red River Hot Springs

By the end of September Magruder had sold out his stock. He got the animals together, rounded up his crew, and headed for Lewiston, trying to beat winter back over the Bitterroots. In Virginia City Magruder picked up an additional hand, 60-year old Billy Page. Page had been prospecting in the Stinking Water when he met Howard (Renton), Lower, and Romain. They introduced him to Magruder, but he knew nothing of their plot. Page was glad for the opportunity to travel with a large party headed west over the mountains.

Through all his trading Magruder had amassed a small fortune, about $18,000, mostly in gold dust, but also in U.S. coin and paper.

The group crossed over the summit on October 6, with occasional snow flurries. On the evening of October 8, after most of the camp was asleep, Lower and Renton were up

Martin Potucek photo

Sign marks the route to the Magruder murder site.

with Magruder, who was on watch; the three chatted amicably. When Magruder reached across the camp fire Lower grabbed an axe and bashed in his skull. Magruder lay dead, face first in the fire. Renton took a swing, too. After that, a systematic slaughter of the rest of the crew followed. Only Page was spared, and he was not sure why.

After collecting the loot, burning what evidence they could, and scattering or shooting any of the mules that followed, the four men headed for Lewiston and points beyond. As they followed the trail down and out of the mountains it occurred to Page that they were depending on him to lead them out and around the main route where they would encounter others. He now thought it poor judgment shooting his mouth off about how well he knew these mountains. They spared him, and even gave him a share of the money, because they needed him.

The robbers skirted Elk City, at about 4,000 ft., moving around the north side of the open valley there. Descending to Newsome Creek, they then climbed out of the drainage of the South Fork of the Clearwater. At a place called Mountain House at 6,000 ft. they stopped for a drink. Crossing another mountain, they now came out Cottonwood Creek to meet the South Fork again. Out through the Camas Prairie, the rough going was behind them. After a failed attempt to cross the high-running Clearwater, they followed an Indian trail toward Lewiston, where they hoped they would be able to find a boat or some way to cross the Snake unnoticed.

They arrived in Lewiston on the evening of October 18, during a storm. From snow and rocky ground they had made it back to civilization in the mud and rain. Early the next day, the four took the stage to Walla Walla. They had come in the night before to buy tickets when Hill Beachy was still at the Luna House, working late. Beachy thought he recognized one of them, but the four names given just didn't smell right. He had two friends that were also heading out on the same stage, and Beachy warned them to be on their guard.

Beachy supposedly had a dream weeks before that froze his soul. He dreamed he saw his friend, Lloyd Magruder lighting his pipe over a fire, and then someone rising up behind him and killing him with the blow of an axe. He shared this vision only with his wife, who advised him not to try and pass it on to his friend. What struck him now was that the face behind the axe was the same as the man buying tickets for the stage. The stage had left. Beachy felt he must do something.

The creeping suspicion that his dream had come true led Beachy to search for some way to learn Magruder's fate. When Magruder's shotgun and mule showed up in one of the stables, that confirmed everything to Beachy. He convinced the sheriff to swear out a warrant for Magruder's murder as volunteers went to Elk City to seek word of Magruder and his men. Beachy, along with a man named Thomas Farrell, and armed with papers signed by the acting governor of the territory, took off west in pursuit of the four suspects.

Because they left Lewiston on the stage for Walla Walla, Beachy surmised the suspects were headed for the Columbia River, which, with its system of steam riverboats, was the main avenue out of the area. At Portland, he just missed the fugitives, but he verified their destination as San Francisco. Beachy was able to telegraph the police in San Francisco to intercept the men. Beachy was able to convince California Governor Leland Stanford, that justice would be served the four back in the new territory of Idaho.

With the help of the police and the Army, the four were escorted back to Lewiston in chains. Beachy's word and duty was to see that the murderers stood trial in Lewiston, as a first test of Idaho's criminal justice system, and not meet their collective fates at the hands of a lynch mob. At the beginning of December, 1863, Beachy, along with four Army guards returned to Lewiston. An excited crowd was there to meet them, and some say a lynching was narrowly averted.

On January 22, 1864, mainly on the testimony of William Page, a territorial jury found Lower, Renton and Romain guilty of the murders of Lloyd Magruder and four others. On the morning of March 4, from a gallows in a small glen just out of Lewiston, the three dropped into hell at the same moment. It was a large crowd that watched, including some Nez Perce, who had never witnessed this sort of white man's justice.

Martin Potucek photo

View from Dry Saddle, looking west.

Significance: Not only was this Idaho's first legal execution, it was a test of the new territory's determination to exist as a lawful entity. The need for a criminal justice code and for law enforcement became an important issue. News of the crime, the chase, the trial, and the execution spread far and wide across the west. Due to the ongoing carnage of the Civil War, the murder of Lloyd Magruder and his party was merely a blip on the horizon to those east of the Great Plains.

If You Want to Go

These directions to follow the Magruder Corridor will go west to east. We'll start from Grangeville, Idaho, and end at Darby, Montana. Warning! Beyond Highway 14 the road may not be plowed, and no services exist for almost 100 miles. Be prepared with plenty of fuel, food, and emergency gear. A Nez Perce National Forest map is also advised, as is the Magruder brochure and checking out the local weather and road conditions with folks at the Red River guard station. Because elevations reach over 8,000 ft., snow can fall at any time. Although a four-wheel-drive vehicle is not necessary, it may well come in handy. Low clearance vehicles, trailers, and motor homes should not venture onto Forest Road 468, the Magruder Corridor Road.

From Grangeville on U.S. Highway 95 travel east on Highway 13. Then go south (right) on Highway 14 as it follows the South Fork of the Clearwater upstream. Near Elk City, Highway 14's eastern end, proceed south on the Mother Lode Road (Forest Road 222) which crosses the American River and then follows the Red River south and eastward. In about fourteen miles the Red River Road (FR 234) leads left to Red River Hot Springs and campgrounds. The developed hot springs are a great place to soak, and the nearby campground at Bridge Creek is convenient.

Adventure detour:

If you're up for a demanding (mountain) bike ride, check out Trail 541 that climbs east from the end of FR 1166 just south of the hot springs. This trail climbs over 2,000 ft. between the tops of Little Green Mountain and Green Mountain at over 7,000 ft. elevation. It connects to the Magruder Corridor Road at Poet Creek Campground about ten miles southeast of the hot springs. To connect to Trail 502, which leads to Poet Creek Campground, just take a left (east) on FR 285 as you come off the top of Green Mountain heading west on the Lookout road; this road will lead you down to 468, west of the campground. If you want an extreme downhill bike ride, proceed on 285 left (NE) less than a mile and a half, and then turn right (south) onto 502. It's an old pack trail that drops down the Green Creek drainage before it spills into Poet Creek. About a half mile

Martin Potucek photo
Deep Creek Bridge (built by CCC during the 1930s). Deep Creek spills into the Selway River on right. Magruder Guard Station is one-half mile south.

north of the campground Hot Springs Creek joins Poet Creek. This last option has some very steep descents and should only be attempted by experts. Beware that there are some older pack trails that connect with the main trail on the ascent to Green Mountain, and there are a few steep sections, but they're not steep for long. This is an experts only ride; carry plenty of water and a topo map before setting off.

Resuming our main trip east to the Magruder Corridor, just past the turnoff to Red River Hot Springs is the Red River Ranger Station. Going right (south) here leads you onto Forest Road 468, which is the Magruder Corridor Road. It follows the old South Nez Perce Trail (which generally runs just north of 468), and it leads all the way to Montana and the Bitterroot Valley. If you're setting off on the corridor road to make the entire traverse across the Bitterroot Range, check in with the local rangers; find out

Martin Potucek photo

Westbound on Magruder Corridor.

about road conditions, weather, or fires. Above all, be prepared to spend the night out, even if you're not planning it. You'll be going over 8,000 ft elevation.

To follow the route all the way to Montana just go left (east) on Forest Road 468, just a short distance south of the Red River Ranger Station off 222; a large sign points the way. For great detailed maps with highlights along the route, get the Magruder Corridor Brochure that's free from any of the Nez Perce or Bitterroot National Forest facilities. All the attractions, hazards, and digressions for this section of road could fill a book in itself. Consider this one of the most rugged and pristine motor routes over our western mountains.

Don't be afraid to venture off on the many trails that are accessible from the corridor road to foot and horse travel. But remember, the wilderness areas to the north and south don't allow mechanized travel of any kind, including bicycles.

Some Highlights of the Magruder Corridor (going west to east)

- Granite Spring Campground
- Poet Creek Campground
- Dry Saddle Campground
- Horse Heaven: saddle and cabin
- Salmon Mountain Lookout Trail
- Sabe Saddle and Vista
- Summit at almost 8200' just north of Salmon Mountain Lookout Trail
- Magruder Campground and Bridge over Selway River
- Magruder massacre site by Beaver Point, one mile north of Magruder Campground
- Magruder Guard Station just south over Deep Creek
- Deep Creek Canyon, Bridge, and Campground
- Nez Perce Pass, Idaho-Montana border (a mile north of here is where the old Indian trail split north and south)
- Fales Flat Campground
- West Fork Ranger Station

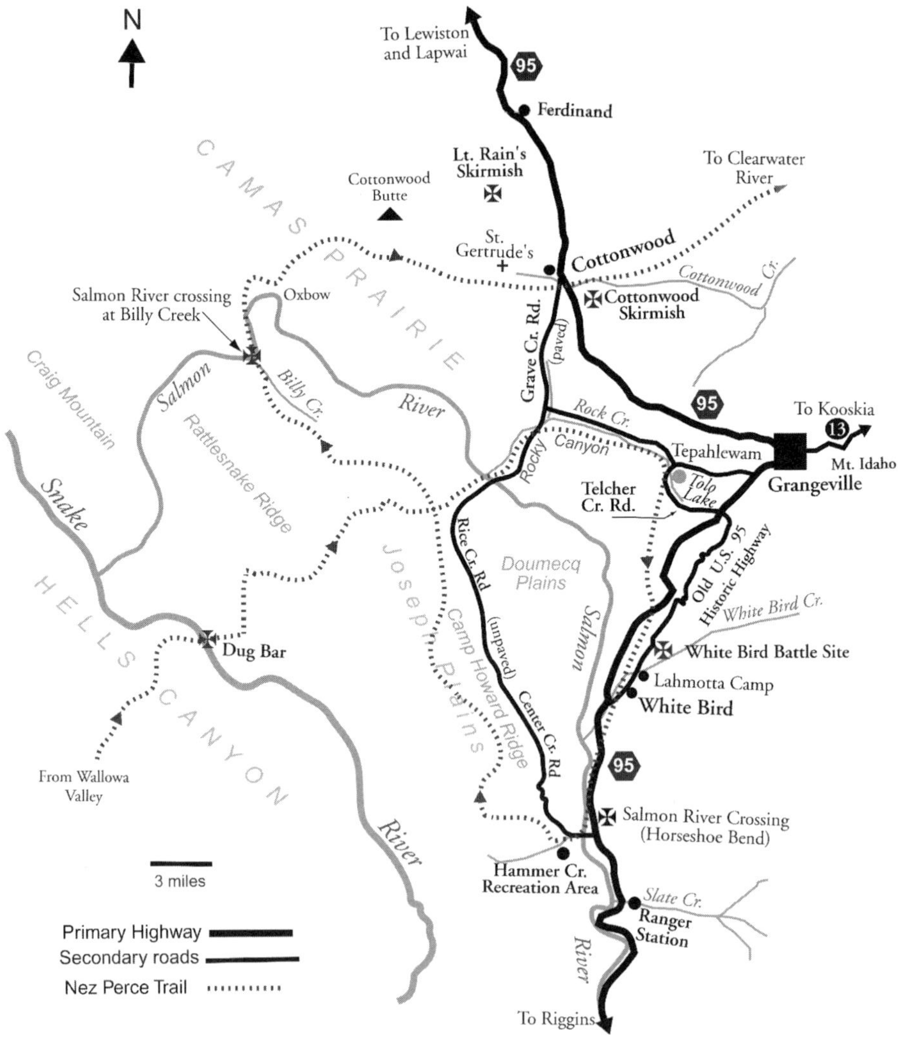
N
To Lewiston and Lapwai
95
Ferdinand
Lt. Rain's Skirmish
Cottonwood Butte
To Clearwater River
CAMAS PRAIRIE
St. Gertrude's
Cottonwood
Cottonwood Cr.
Cottonwood Skirmish
Salmon River crossing at Billy Creek
Oxbow
Grave Cr. Rd.
(paved)
Craig Mountain
Salmon
Billy Cr.
River
Rock Cr.
To Kooskia
13
Rattlesnake Ridge
Rocky Canyon
Tepahlewam
Mt. Idaho
Grangeville
Snake
Telcher Cr. Rd.
Tolo Lake
Old U.S. 95 Historic Highway
Rice Cr. Rd
Doumecq Plains
Joseph Plains
Camp Howard Ridge
HELLS CANYON
Salmon
White Bird Cr.
Dug Bar
(unpaved)
White Bird Battle Site
Lahmotta Camp
White Bird
Center Cr. Rd
From Wallowa Valley
Salmon River Crossing (Horseshoe Bend)
River
Hammer Cr. Recreation Area
3 miles
Slate Cr.
Ranger Station
Primary Highway
Secondary roads
Nez Perce Trail
River
To Riggins

Chapter Seven

The Nez Perce War

Until the discovery of gold in the Clearwater River country by E. D. Pierce and the following gold rush of 1860, the Nez Perce Indians (the Ni-mi-pu or Nee-Mee-poo) had been friendly with and welcomed the white newcomers. Even though a treaty signed by Washington territorial Governor Isaac Stevens and many Northwest Indian chiefs in 1855 in Walla Walla had set aside that land to protect it from white encroachment, little was done to enforce that treaty.

In 1862 Fort Lapwai was built on Lapwai Creek (at Spalding, now run by the National Park Service), just south of modern day Lewiston. This fort made the Nez Perce suspicious of the whites' intentions, especially after seizures of their lands increased with no response from the military or civil authority.

By 1855 a majority of the tribe opposed any further negotiations with the U. S. government. Looking Glass was an ardent voice for resisting the white encroachment, and for maintaining the traditional culture. He was a well-respected war chief, but was considered too old to lead in battle effectively. Eagle-from-the-Light was young and ambitious, and sought to take over Looking Glass's role and voice. Lawyer, a minor chief whose band lived just south of present day Craigmont, Idaho, opposed resisting the whites. This came to a head at a general council of the Nez Perces in August 1861.

The $50,000 the U.S. Congress was to have appropriated for the purchase of the Nez Perce lands agreed upon in 1855 never materialized. This money, along with help in building a mill, smith shop, barns, and help in establishing a working model farm, was to be payment for the ancestral territory the Indians would be giving up elsewhere. Bitterness followed as Indian commissioners for the government told them in Lapwai in 1862 that payment would be delayed.

In May 1863 a conference of Nez Perce chiefs was called to lay claim to parts of a 10,000 square-mile reservation being set aside for the Nez Perce nation. Eagle-from-the-Light claimed White Bird Creek near the Salmon River; Big Thunder sought the land around the Lapwai agency; Old Joseph took the valleys of the Wallowa and the Imnaha. Lawyer, the flexible diplomat, proposed that his people give up all but about a twentieth of the whole. Old Joseph, for his part, had only signed the 1855 treaty because of the whites' promises of their rights to those areas, which were ancestral and sacred.

Approaching death in 1871, Old Joseph bowed to his oldest son (Tooyalakekt), Young Joseph, as the new diplomatic chief. Although both father and son were peace-loving, the father made the son promise that he would resist the influx of settlers on their ancient tribal grounds, and never give up the Wallowa Valley.

By 1876, white ranchers and farmers demanded that

the government allow them to settle on the prime areas in the Wallowas. It was their contention that since a majority of chiefs had signed the new treaty of 1863, the dissenters, called the non-treaty Nez Perces, had no standing, and must move to the reservation at Lapwai.

Part of the impetus behind this new treaty was that Idaho Territory was established on March 3, 1863. Add to that Oregon's birth as a state in 1859. This created a new sense of ownership and territorial right by the whites of the region. Removing Joseph's band from the Wallowa Valley was a tidy solution because it erased any claim against the new state of Oregon. This put the problem off into Idaho, a newly formed territory with little funds, government in its infancy, and a governor whose whereabouts were unknown.

Lawyer was not without his own agenda at that final treaty meeting in May 1863 at Lapwai. He made a proposal that was signed by the commissioners and himself. That document made him head man of his nation, which by the custom of his own people, was not possible. The other chiefs were discredited as his own status rose. This treaty was to supercede the 1855 agreement, and reduce their lands to 1.5 million acres, down from 6.4 million acres. $260,000 in annual payments and materials were to be made in compensation for this concession. Factor in the demands of the raging Civil War and the low status and great distance of the native peoples of the Northwest, and the total amount paid by Congress was, again, zero. White credibility in the Indians' eyes was taking another slide.

The Nez Perces had not participated in the resistance shown by the Coeur d'Alenes and Spokanes to the north in 1858 or by the Shoshones, Bannocks, and Snakes between 1863 and 1868 to the south. But this pacificism was broken by the rift between the treaty Indians (those who moved onto the Lapwai agency) and the non-treaty Indians (those who refused to do so), who still honored the original 1855 agreement. Most of the Lapwai Nez Perce were Christians while the non-treaty groups were members of the Indian "Dreamer" religion.

On May 3, 1877, General Howard called for a council at Lapwai with the non-reservation Nez Perces. Toohoolhoolzote submitted to the indignity of arrest when he verbally resisted Howard's ultimatum to move onto the reservation at Lapwai. He did this rather than risk starting a war on the spot. Toohoolhoolzote was a member of the Dreamer faith that General Howard thought was responsible for unrest among the natives.

A deadline was given Joseph to evacuate his people and stock, which included hundreds of horses and cattle, and to take their places at the Lapwai agency. That deadline was June 14, 1877. It seemed futile to resist at this point. General Howard had troops garrisoned at Lapwai. The task facing Joseph and his people was to round up their stock that had been let out to winter range. The animals were scattered throughout the dozens of drainages of the Wallowa basin.

After the exhausting roundup, the 6,000 animals (many with new offspring), and hundreds of people, many women and children, all would have to cross the Snake and Salmon Rivers at the highest water of the year. Many of the newborn animals were left with their mothers on the south (west) bank of the Snake, where they crossed at what's now known as Big Eddy, near River Mile 196 upstream from Lewiston. This successful crossing, between the northern end of Hell's Canyon and the Mouth of the Imnaha River, brought Joseph's band to an ancient meeting place on the Camas Prairie by Tolo Lake, in White Bird's territory. Here, they met with four other bands of

Martin Potucek photo

Tolo Lake, a Nez Perce gathering place near Grangeville.

non-treaty Nez Perces. For ten days the five related, but distinct bands celebrated, rested, and participated in games and councils, preparing for an uncertain future.

Joseph's was the largest band, with maybe sixty braves. Joseph was only tribal chief to his own group, and his brother Olikut was the leading warrior and hunter. Joseph himself was the youngest chief of the five bands there.

White Bird's group was the next largest, with perhaps 50 men of warrior status. White Bird, himself, was the oldest of these chiefs, now in his seventies. He had great standing among all of the Nez Perce; his long experience in the buffalo country, as a warrior, and medicine man afforded him great status among his people.

Looking Glass headed the third band present here. His group counted no more than forty full grown men. Their base was on the south fork of the Clearwater River but extended to the crest of the Bitterroot Mountains that divide Idaho from Montana. Looking Glass had earned a great reputation as a war chief by helping the Crows in buffalo country defeat the Sioux in a tribal war.

Toohoolhollzote was the leader of the fourth band, with perhaps thirty warriors. He was known as a fierce and powerful hunter and fighter, perhaps the strongest of the entire group of Indians gathered here. However, he did not want war with the whites.

The last group was a fragment of Palouses (related to the Nez Perce). Their leaders, Hahtalekin and Huishuiskute, lived along the Snake River. They comprised only sixteen warriors. Huishuiskute was also a Dreamer, and he, too was on Howard's list of persona non gratis.

All was progressing well, and to all appearances, Joseph's band was moving toward their new home. The total of these five bands was perhaps 500, including women, children, and the elderly; less than 200 could be considered warriors. In the meantime, by early May, Howard had sent a detachment of more than 100 cavalry and a Gatling gun, under the command of Captain S. G. Whipple, to reinforce the army's position in the Wallowa Valley.

On June 13, the five bands were camped at Te-pah-le-wam, near Tolo Lake, just west of present-day Grangeville. They staged a parade, a sort of tribute to their traditional way of life that was due to end on the next day, when they were due to arrive at Lapwai. An insult from a brave to a younger member of White Bird's band at this ceremony started a crucial chain of events in play. Yellow Grizzly Bear shouted to Wahlitits, after his horse had trampled some drying roots, that the young brave would do better to avenge his father's death than play brave in the parade.

Wayne Cornell photo
Hayfield off U.S. 95 at John Day Creek where Henry Elfers was killed.

What the older warrior referred to was an incident years earlier at the mouth of White Bird Creek on the Salmon River. Eagle Robe, Wahlitits's father had allowed a white by the name of Larry Ott to settle on a plot of ground near his home, making him promise to stay off his garden plot. Ott gradually took more and more ground until he built a fence across the Indian's land intending to keep him from it. Eagle Robe protested; an argument followed. Ott then shot the unarmed Indian. As Wahlitits held his dying father, his last request was for him not to avenge his death, to "Let him live his life!" And the son had had always respected his father's wish, until this taunt by the older brave.

Yellow Grizzly Bear's words were a challenge. Wahlitits and two other teenagers headed out the next morning for Ott's cabin. Ott was not home; some accounts say that he fled when he heard of Indians at the nearby encampment. They did find Richard Devine, however. His reputation as an Indian hater had been recently cemented by setting his

Martin Potucek photo
French Cemetery near Salmon River and White Bird.

dogs on Nez Perces passing by and threatening them with his rifle. Surprising him in his cabin, the young braves killed him and took his gun, ammunition, and a horse. A short distance down the Salmon River they found another white, Henry Elfers. He, too had a history of antagonism with the Nez Perce. He also was killed.

The young warriors returned to camp, but stopped short of riding all the way in. They sent the youngest, who knew nothing of Wahlitits's purpose when they set out, to tell White Bird's band what they had done. This was done apparently to show the tribe that they were responsible for the killings, and not the band as a whole. The other reason for staying out of camp but nearby was to invite other warriors who might want to join them in resisting the whites as rulers. The next morning sixteen more young warriors joined them.

Joseph had no knowledge of what had taken place; he

was off slaughtering and packing beef for the final ride to Lapwai and his wife was expecting a baby. When a rider finally did bring word of what had happened, Joseph and his brother Olikut rode back to camp to find everyone packing up and getting ready to flee. They tried to reason with those preparing to run, saying it was better to stay, explain, and work "to make some kind of peace."

Looking Glass and his band headed for the South Fork of the Clearwater, followed by the Palouses. Most of Joseph's band also were unwilling to join in the fight; this left only a small band of Nez Perces, under twenty, who would terrorize the countryside the next few days. But word spread fast, first to the white settlements at Mount Idaho, and then to Lapwai and Walla Walla. Before a single soldier was involved, by June 14, 1877, a full scale Indian war had broken out.

Arthur I. (Ad) Chapman sent word from Mount Idaho, where settlers were massing and preparing to defend themselves, to Fort Lapwai, calling for help from the army. General Howard was there already to oversee the non-treaty Indians settling in to the reservation there. Only two companies of soldiers were garrisoned there at the time. Upon hearing of the violence moving up from the Salmon River, he sent Captain Perry with a company (about 100 men) to march immediately to Mount Idaho. They left at 10 p.m. and rode all night.

Stopping at Cottonwood at the Norton Ranch to rest and eat, the soldiers were joined by some volunteers from Mount Idaho. Chapman, a hothead and the same man who had sent for help, headed the eleven volunteers. He was to accompany Perry because he knew the land toward White Bird well, while Perry had never been there. Chapman was married to a Nez Perce woman but had a quick temper and was not held in high regard by the Indians

Martin Potucek photo
White Bird battlefield today, looking upslope (north) from Nez Perce positions, toward bluffs where soldiers halted their advance.

On June 17, 1877, at about 2 a.m. Perry's force entered White Bird Canyon, and began descending the steep grade, planning on catching the renegades by surprise. Having ridden over seventy miles in less than thirty hours across heavily timbered and steep terrain, Perry's men were pushed to the point of exhaustion. Many were green (had never seen action), and the volunteers lacked discipline and training. About an hour before sunrise, they came close to the vicinity of the Nez Perce camp, just above White Bird Creek. Three unarmed Nez Perce scouts led with a small advanced guard of soldiers shortly behind. Perry proceeded cautiously, sensing the exposed position he was entering; high rock walls towered above to their west, while curious knobs rose downslope.

Ollicott, a great fighter and leader during times of war, urged his warriors to remember the standing Nez Perce

Martin Potucek photo

Swartz Pond at White Bird battlefield, looking south. Indian camp was located at the bottom of the canyon in the middle right portion of the photo.

order, never fire the first shot. This was to assure the tribe, when it came to confrontation, that there was no other way out. The Indian leaders had sent six warriors to meet the soldiers; a white flag of truce was held high, showing that they wished to talk.

Chapman was with the advanced guard, under the command of Lieutenant Theller. Also along with these eight men was a bugler; his job was to signal Theller's commands to the main force. The Indian scouts halted when they spotted the peace party. Chapman overran them and saw them, too. What possessed him at this point is anyone's guess. He charged ahead on his horse firing a couple of shots from his rifle. Perhaps twenty soldiers followed closely. The Indian peace party heard the shots and saw the charge, complete with bugler calling orders loudly. About a hundred yards away, one of the older warriors in

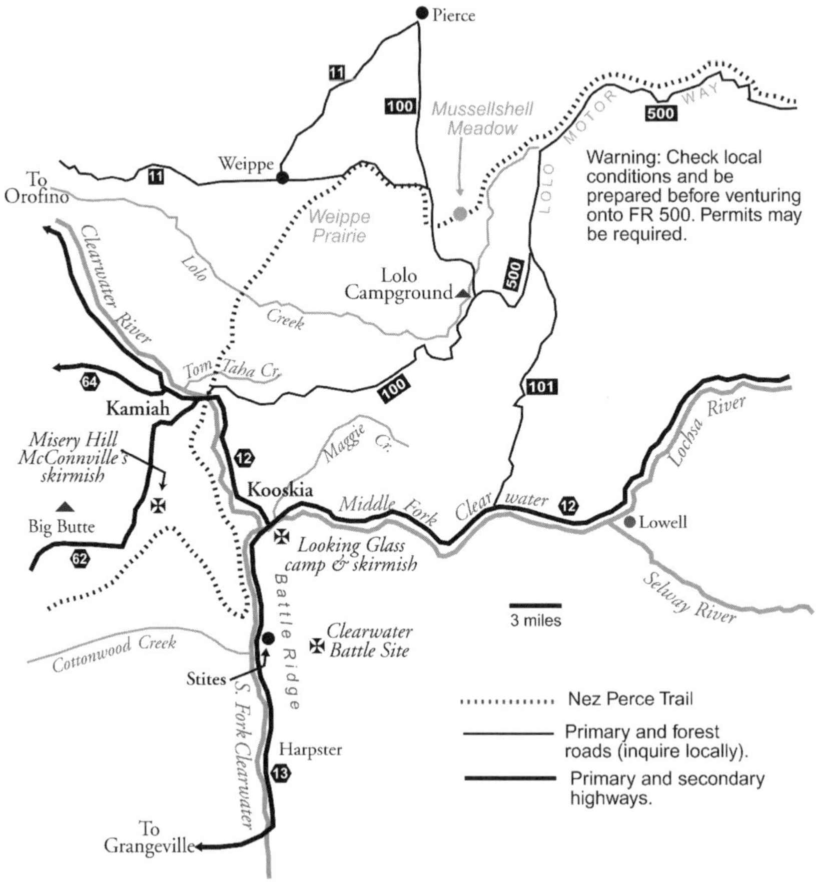
Pierce
11
100
Mussellshell Meadow
LOLO MOTOR WAY
500
Weippe
To Orofino
Weippe Prairie
Warning: Check local conditions and be prepared before venturing onto FR 500. Permits may be required.
Lolo Creek
Lolo Campground
Clearwater River
Tom Taha Cr.
64
Kamiah
101
Misery Hill McConnville's skirmish
12
Maggie Cr.
Lochsa River
Kooskia
Middle Fork Clearwater
Big Butte
Lowell
62
Looking Glass camp & skirmish
Battle Ridge
Selway River
3 miles
Clearwater Battle Site
Cottonwood Creek
Stites
S. Fork Clearwater
Harpster
13
To Grangeville
Nez Perce Trail
Primary and forest roads (inquire locally).
Primary and secondary highways.

the peace party was Otstotpoo. He turned to the others beside him and told them to watch as he would shoot the bugler. In a moment, the bugler dropped dead from his saddle. Seeing this, Chapman and the other charging soldiers whirled around and high-tailed it back to the main force.

The soldiers, without their bugler to convey commands above the din of battle, were unable to act in a coordinated way. The planned surprise attack would turn out to be a surprise for those who planned it. By 7 a.m. barely two hours after it had begun, thirty-four soldiers lay dead and two wounded. The Nez Perce suffered not one loss, with only three slightly wounded. The Indians chased the survivors to the ouskirts of Grangeville. Less than fifty warriors took part in the battle, although they were strategically positioned. Later, General Howard would tell the world that over 500 warriors had participated in the "massacre." It came to be one of the best known Indian humiliations of the U.S. Army, after Custer's defeat the year before at Little Big Horn.

White Bird and young Joseph's brother, Ollicott, led the two bands of Nez Perce above White Bird Creek and toward the Salmon River. This was White Bird's ancestral home, and he was leaving it now with his band, Joseph's band, and thousands of head of horses and cattle. Of the few hundred Indians who comprised the combined band, less than a third were warriors; the rest were women, children, and the elderly. White Bird and Joseph decided quickly after the battle, which was a defensive effort to protect their camp from his surprise attack, that retreating west across the Salmon River was their best course of action.

A week later, General Howard arrived at the scene of the battle with 500 men, two Gatling guns, a small howitzer, and a pack train. After burying the dead, they proceeded with great difficulty to cross the Salmon River near Slate Creek. From there, the bands turned northwest over Dolimecq and Joseph Plains, then dropped down to recross the Salmon at the old Craig Billy crossing just west of the Oxbow. Essentially, the tribes were doubling back in a big loop to the Camas Prairie. They knew the crossing back down river would be difficult for the soldiers. Following the Indians' track down the Salmon, the soldiers tried to follow them, but failed completely in recrossing. Howard's force then retraced their path all the way back over White Bird Pass, and returned to Grangeville on July 8. They had spent two weeks chasing their prey and had achieved nothing. The Nez Perce had gained more precious time.

Once again, Ad Chapman played a pivotal role when he took Chief Looking Glass's confidence and betrayed it. The chief had told Chapman, toward the end of June, by his camp on the South Fork of the Clearwater River and some fifty miles northeast of White Bird, of the non-treaties' break away. Howard then received news that Looking Glass had been supplying Joseph's renegades with warriors, and so he sent Captain Whipple to round up Looking Glass's band and imprison them at Cottonwood under the care of Chapman. After attacking Looking Glass's unsuspecting group, which resulted in the death of an Indian mother and child and the capture of a herd of horses, Looking Glass fled with his people to join Joseph and White Bird. He also vowed "as long as I live I will never make peace with the treacherous Americans. I am ready for war."

On July 5, Captain Whipple returned with his force to Cottonwood where they encamped. Looking for the Indians, he sent two white scouts west. When only one returned, barely escaping a Nez Perce war party, he sent out a small detachment of a dozen men headed by

Wayne Cornell photo
Rocks northwest of Cottonwood where a dozen soldiers lead by Lieutenant S. M. Rains was wiped out by Nez Perce warriors

Lieutenant S. M. Rains. Whipple wanted more information on the location and strength of the Indians. They headed west, and before long, encountered the main force of Joseph's warriors. After a quick skirmish and a retreat into some rocks by the surviving half dozen troopers, the remainder of Rains' force was wiped out.

On July 4, Captain Perry was leading a lightly escorted packtrain of supplies and ammunition from Lapwai to Cottonwood, hoping to find Howard's main force. Instead, he met Captain Whipple, who apprised him of Howard's pursuit of the Indians. He immediately set his men to work digging trenches for defense.

At this time Captain D. B. Randall had organized a group of sixteen armed volunteers from Mt. Idaho; they were marching toward Cottonwood to join the soldiers there. Less than two miles from Cottonwood on the wagon road, and in sight of the soldiers' camp, a band of Nez

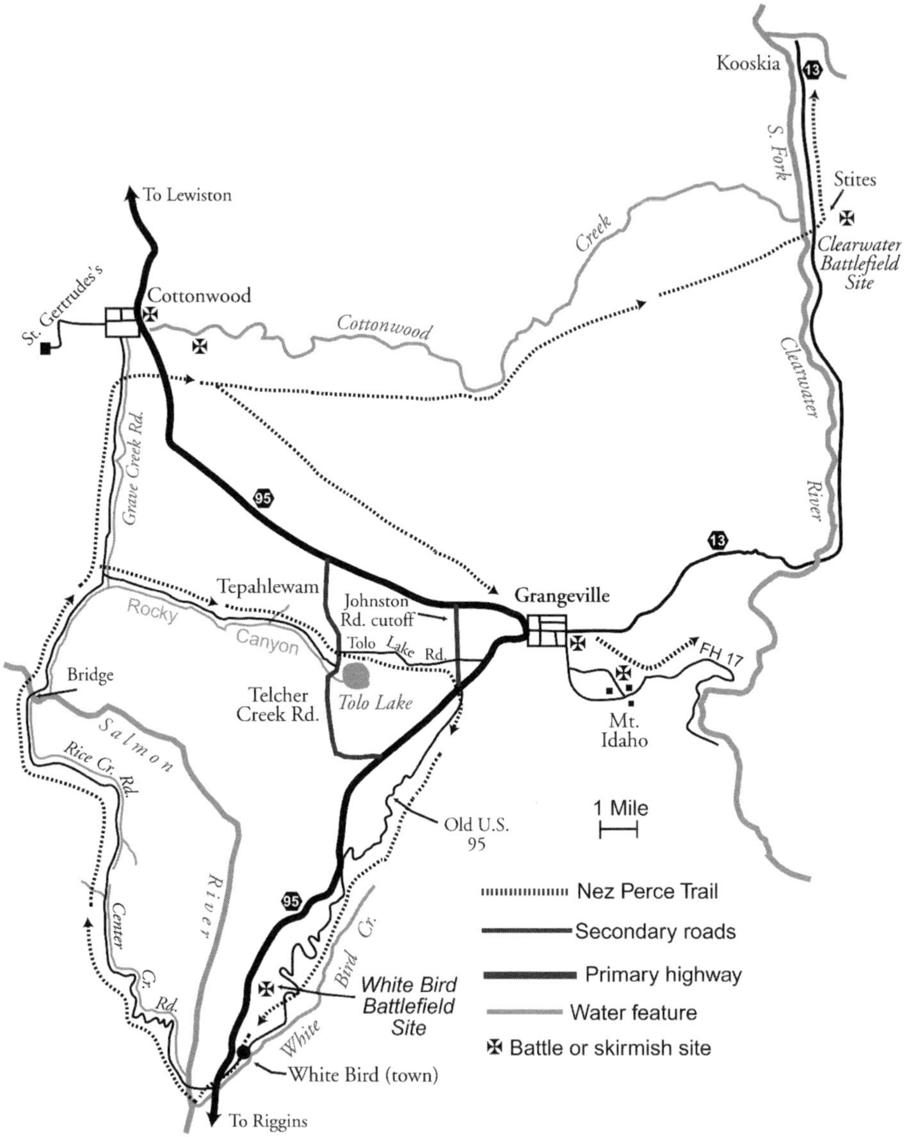
To Lewiston
St. Gertrudes's
Cottonwood
Cottonwood
Creek
Kooskia
S. Fork
Stites
Clearwater Battlefield Site
Clearwater
River
Grave Creek Rd.
95
13
Tepahlewam
Rocky
Canyon
Johnston Rd. cutoff
Grangeville
Tolo Lake Rd.
FH 17
Bridge
Telcher Creek Rd.
Tolo Lake
Mt. Idaho
Salmon
Rice Cr. Rd.
Old U.S. 95
1 Mile
River
Center Cr. Rd.
95
Bird Cr.
White
White Bird Battlefield Site
White Bird (town)
To Riggins
Nez Perce Trail
Secondary roads
Primary highway
Water feature
Battle or skirmish site

Martin Potucek photo
East end of Clearwater battlefield, on plateau above Stites, Idaho. Nez Perce rifle pits are still visible at left.

Perce warriors met the volunteer force. A battle ensued, lasting several hours. Captain Perry was charged with cowardice later, because he hesitated in sending help to the volunteers, who were visible from the army positions at Cottonwood. Finally, he sent help, and the Indians retreated, but not after Randall and another were killed. The first Nez Perce warrior also died in this skirmish of what was now being called the Nez Perce War.

The main Indian force moved east across the Camas Prairie toward the juncture of the main forks of the Clearwater River. They did not need to hurry now, for they knew that Howard's force would still be days in back-tracking from their inability to recross the Snake River by Craig's Ferry.

Led by Ad Chapman, Howard brought a force of infantry, cavalry, and artillery to a spot Chapman thought Joseph's group would camp. This was just south of where Looking Glass's village was destroyed by Whipple. Chapman was off by miles, but that only delayed Howard's attack. The Battle of the Clearwater had begun. Because of the location of the Indian camp, Howard could not use his cannon or Gattling guns effectively. The battlefront was strung out over two miles, and it lasted two days, July 11-12, with neither side mounting a serious charge on the other. Too-hool-hool-zote and a couple dozen sharp shooters were able to harry their enemies from changing positions and keep the soldiers at bay.

The Battle of the Clearwater was indecisive; the Nez Perce broke camp and moved north toward Kamiah, leaving many possessions behind. The army lost fifteen men and twenty-seven wounded while the non-treaties lost four with five wounded. That did not prevent Howard from reporting to the press, which were greedily conveying the struggle to the American public, that he had "a most important success" and that the Indians were "in full flight." From his Civil War experience, Howard understood well the importance of good press.

Now the group of 650 (250 warriors, the rest women, children, and elderly) and more than 2,000 animals crossed the Clearwater River. As usual, this was accomplished by stretching buffalo hides across circular frames made of willow or other limber branches. Howard's force actually caught up to them after they had crossed, but once again, lacking the skills to quickly cross a swift running river, the pursuers were forced to backtrack half a day to Dunwell's Ferry downstream. That meant a half day back upstream and more time lost to the army.

Keep in mind that after the Battle of the Clearwater the united bands fled in mostly family units, collecting and gathering members who were spread out across the creeks and hollows, sometimes miles apart. They did not move in a linear procession like their enemy. They would regroup from place to place. Looking Glass was camped on the west bank of the South Fork of the Clearwater here, by the mouth of Cottonwood Creek with four other bands, when the army attacked from the heights on the east side. That was July 11 when the army cut loose with gattling guns and howitzers. After a full day of pitched battle, the bands were able to flee north up the east side of the South Fork until it meets the main Clearwater at Kamiah.

Local sources say the flight of the non treaty Nez Perce generally followed the two steep ridges either side of Tom Taha Creek (the creek itself was choked with brush). This steep creek bottom is really a canyon in most places as it rises over 2,000 feet directly east of Kamiah. From here, the group traveled east and north to the Weippe Praire, an ancient camas gathering site and summer camp for the Nez Perce, near the spot where the tribe first met members of the Lewis and Clark Expedition, seventy years earlier.

On July 15, at the camas grounds the hostiles met a band of Nez Perce returning from the buffalo country. When Red Heart, leader of the forty-five Indians, heard of their plight, he wanted nothing to do with the conflict, so he led his people toward Lapwai, planning on avoiding it. That was not to be, for when Howard encountered them, he took their horses and possessions and marched them on foot sixty miles to Fort Lapwai where they were imprisoned. It wasn't until the following April that the grown men and some family members were released from Fort Vancouver, down on the Columbia River, and sent home. A just reward? Howard reported to the press of his capture of a large group of warriors.

The hostiles called a council at Weippe to decide what course to take. It was decided to cross the Bitterroot Mountains over the Lolo Trail. Lolo is an ancient word, meaning to carry. Once into the buffalo country, they could head north to Canada, where Sitting Bull, the Sioux leader at Little Big Horn the year before, had fled, or they could

Potucek photo
Musselshell Meadow, east of Weippe. Here the Nez Perces held a council where they decided to move east over the mountains to Montana.

go south to their friends, the Crows, toward Yellowstone. Joseph did not want to flee the ancestral homelands at all. In the end, Looking Glass was chosen as leader at this point, for he was the eldest and knew the buffalo country well; it was his will that won out, to cross the mountains and go south to Crow country, to their friends.

On July 16, the Nez Perce headed east on the Lolo Trail; it was an ancient route used for generations to cross the Bitterroots into the summer grazing lands of the buffalo. A rear guard of five young warriors was left behind to track the army's pursuit. An advanced guard of Christian Nez Perce scouts was sent ahead by Howard to determine his foe's actions. A skirmish between these two guards left one scout for Howard dead; his crime was not heeding previous warnings by his former fellow tribesmen not to work for the army against his own people.

The Nez Perce crossed the mountains along the thin, steep, and heavily forested trail in six days; a remarkable achievement. The ancient trail had been improved in 1866 to promote commerce between Lewiston and the gold fields of Montana. (To see their route across the mountains, look at the Lolo Trail map in the Lewis and Clark chapter. The Corps of Discovery essentially followed the northern Nez Perce Trail (Lolo Trail) out and back across the Bitterroots.) Howard's troops, following the same line, took about twice the time, cutting down trees, moving fallen logs, and finding the entire route one big struggle. The Indians knew this would happen, and so when they crossed to the eastern slope, they eased their pace.

Howard's force, by the time it arrived in Montana, was a full week behind its quarry. There was even the feeling that Howard might not follow, for this was Montana territory (a different army department). This was not to be the case. After an aborted attempt to stop them by a few dozen soldiers from Missoula and some citizen volunteers at the mouth of Lolo Canyon (Fort Fizzle), the Nez Perce proceeded unmolested south up the Bitterroot Valley.

During the next two months, the non-treaty bands stayed just ahead of Howard's force and the converging forces of other army units in Montana. They would be surprised at the Battle of Big Hole and suffer their first real casualties there. And, although a handful would escape to Canada, the surviving non-treaty Nez Perce would succumb to defeat near the Bear Paw Mountains in northern Montana. Joseph, himself, was never allowed to return to his Wallowa homeland.

If You Want to Go

Following the exact route of the Nez Perce as they were pursued by Howard is almost impossible these days. Some places are well known and easily accessible; others are only faint traces that are now choked with brush. The area below Hells Canyon is some of the most rugged and diffi-

Martin Potucek photo
Mammoth replica at Grangeville. Skeleton taken from Tolo Lake.

cult up-and-down country on the continent, and the Nee-me-poo knew this. Some modern roads and trails have been developed in places, but none closely follow their path except the Lolo Trail east of Weippe.

Joseph's band moved from the Wallowa Valley in northeastern Oregon, in spring of 1877, down the Imnaha River to a place on the Snake River known as Dug Bar. You can get to Dug Bar (which is a dead end) on the west side of the Snake by starting from Imnaha, Oregon, northeast of Enterprise. Take Lower Imnaha Road north, following the Imnaha River. It turns into Forest Road 4260 and winds around the west side of Cactus Mountain. It then drops down to Dug Bar on the Snake. Crossing the Snake is possible with a boat or by swimming at this point. For a more leisurely trip, take Highway 3 north out of Enterprise toward Lewiston, Idaho.

From the town of Whitebird, Idaho, just off U.S, Highway 95, you can follow the general course of the Nez Perce flight in 1877 all the way to Montana, at Lolo Pass. The easiest motor route takes U.S. 95 north (past the Whitebird Battle site just up the grade) toward Grangeville. A variation of this follows the old highway, now the paved park battlefield road which winds just east of the main highway from Whitebird Canyon all the way to the summit of Whitebird Hill and beyond.

Adventure Option

An adventurous option, not recommended for trailers or motorhomes, is to cross the Salmon River to the Hammer Creek Recreation Area off of U.S. 95 near Whitebird. This option is rugged in places, and may not be passable year-round, but it follows the Nez Perce's trail more accurately. You can resume the main motor route by backtracking from Cottonwood to Grangeville via U.S. 95. From Hammer Creek you can follow the Center Creek Road (steep, winding, gravel, as it climbs over 2,000 ft.) north to the Rice Creek Road, which drops down off of Doumecq Plains and recrosses the Salmon over the Rice Creek Bridge.

About a half mile off the highway, you can park at some dumptsers on the right and follow a short trail to where some settlers graves are located behind a split rail fence. The Mason family is buried here, victims of the young renegade band and its deadly vengeance which became the spark that ignited the Nez Perce War. Just follow the wide paved road as it turns to gravel after Hammer Creek. At the top of the ridge, turn right at the unmarked fork, which brings you down Rice Creek. Cross the one lane bridge over the Salmon and go left at the split just after the bridge. Going right takes you to Pine Bar on the Salmon.

From here you can follow the Rocky Canyon Road north and then go left (north again) onto the Grave Creek Road, which turns to pavement as it splits off from Rock Creek. Note that the private road to the right follows Rocky Canyon (Rock Creek); that is the ancient route the Nee-Me-Poo took to Tepahlewam by Tolo Lake, where the early summer gatherings of the widespread bands took place. Be sure to stop by the Weis Rock Shelter, a prehistoric site on the

Grave Creek Road, just a mile up from the Rocky Canyon fork. Ancestors of the Nez Perce are said to have inhabited this site almost continuously for the past 8,000 years. This part of the loop is quite imposing: basalt walls form roofs and caves looming over the roadway, sometimes reaching hundreds of feet in height. It's easy to feel the ancient legacy of this place.

Turn right (east) on Twin House Road (the first paved road right, off the Grave Creek road after it rises up onto the Camas Prairie); this will return you to Highway 95 south of Cottonwood to resume our main tour back at Grangeville (right). Special Note: Just east of Cottonwood (going straight or north on the Grave Creek Road) a few miles is St. Gertrude's Museum, where you can see a Nez Perce exhibit.

End Adventure Loop: resume main tour at Grangeville.

From the top of Whitebird Hill, U.S. 95 drops down to the Camas Prairie. Taking the Johnston Road west (left) a few miles before Grangeville and then the first paved road left will take you in a few miles to the ancient summer gathering site of the Nez Perce. The Nee-Mee-Poo would come here to Tolo Lake (the area was known as Tepahlewam) up from the Salmon River just west through Rocky Canyon, which is just hidden from view at the lake. This is also the site where, in 1994 while the lake was drained for excavation work, a Columbian Mammoth skeleton was found. Its replica is housed just off the highway in Grangeville for all to see. It's estimated that there are 200 or more like it still there, along with ancient bison.

To continue the general route, go right (east) off of Highway 95 through Grangeville and onto Highway 13 heading east; this will take you to the South Fork of the Clearwater River, which flows north to Kooskia. Mount

Idaho is the small community just a few miles southeast of Grangeville where the local settlers of 1877 retreated to and stockaded themselves early that summer.

Martin Potucek photo
Weis Rockshelter near Cottonwood.

On Highway 13 just before Cottonwood Creek's confluence with the Clearwater at the town of Stites is the marked site of the Clearwater Battlefield. Recent improvements by the Park Service should highlight details of the battle by 2003. The battle started with troops attacking from the heights above (east) the Nez Perce camp across the river (west). The attackers were stopped at the canyon rim and forced to entrench on the plateau. The upper end of the battle site can be found by taking the Stites Canyon Road at the south end of Stites. It starts as pavement as it climbs steeply through the canyon, and then turns to gravel as you go right and up onto the plateau. In less than another mile, go right onto a dirt road just past a metal silo. Go another 100 yards and stop at the fence by an old crabapple tree. Walking about 200 yards west (back toward the river) and just below the rim, you'll find the old rifle pits (crescent-shaped basalt rock piles) used in the battle. Note: This area is accessible only with permission at this point in time. It may or may not be opened to the general public in the future. This is tribal land being operated by a leaseholder; please respect this as private property and as hallowed ground. *End option.*

Resume our route on Highway 13 north to where it ends at its junction with U.S. 12 on the north side of the Middle Fork of the Clearwater (the South Fork joins it here). Follow Highway 12 left to the town of Kamiah. Just a couple of miles before Kamiah is a Nez Perce National Historic Park site: the Heart of the Monster, the traditional creation place of the Nee-Me-Poo. A half mile past on the river are historic markers for Lewis and Clark's Long Camp and Asa Smith's 1837 mission to the Nez Perce.

The best guess the trail the Nez Perce followed beyond Kooskia is not a trail at all; it ascends the two ridges either side of Tom Taha Creek east and north out of Kamiah and onto the Weippe Prairie at the upper end of Incendiary Creek. From the prairie, the most likely course was through Musselshell Meadows and onto the high trail.

At Kamiah, U.S. 12 crosses the Clearwater to the west side and follows the river toward Lewiston. About a dozen miles farther on this route will take you to Greer and the junction of Highway 11 which winds up and east to Weippe. From Weippe you can access the Lolo Trail, the route the Nee-Mee-Poo took over the mountains. Just go straight at the four-way intersection in Weippe as Highway 11 turns left (north) towards Pierce. By going straight, you're following Pierce Street to the east. Eight miles east of Weippe turn right onto Forest Road 100, heading south. Just stay on FR 100 as it turns to pavement. Consider stopping at Musselshell Meadows on the left where there's a short trail to an interpretive area. FR 100 now descends into the Lolo Creek drainage where you can access Forest Road 500 (Lolo Motorway) east all the way to Lolo Pass. Read the note below before attempting it. To return to Kamiah and Highway 12, just continue on FR100 west.

Adventure Option

A more adventurous and accurate option is to follow Forest Road 100 east off of U.S. 12 just north of Kamiah; the junction for this road is on the east side of the river before the Clearwater bridge. It starts out as Woodland Road, as it follows the river downstream, then within a mile, it climbs steeply up Tom Taha Creek. This option brings you up Lolo Creek toward Weippe. By taking FR 500 (Lolo Motorway) right (east) from its junction near Bradford Bridge, you can follow their approximate path all the way to Montana. Be prepared, and plan an all day trip. End option.

Because there is such a good chance to get confused, get advice in Kamiah before going off the main highway. And if you're considering heading up the Lolo Trail, remember: It's a full day trip with no services for over seventy miles. Be prepared. Special permits will be required to travel the Lolo Motorway between 2003 and 2006 and travel may be one-way (east to west).

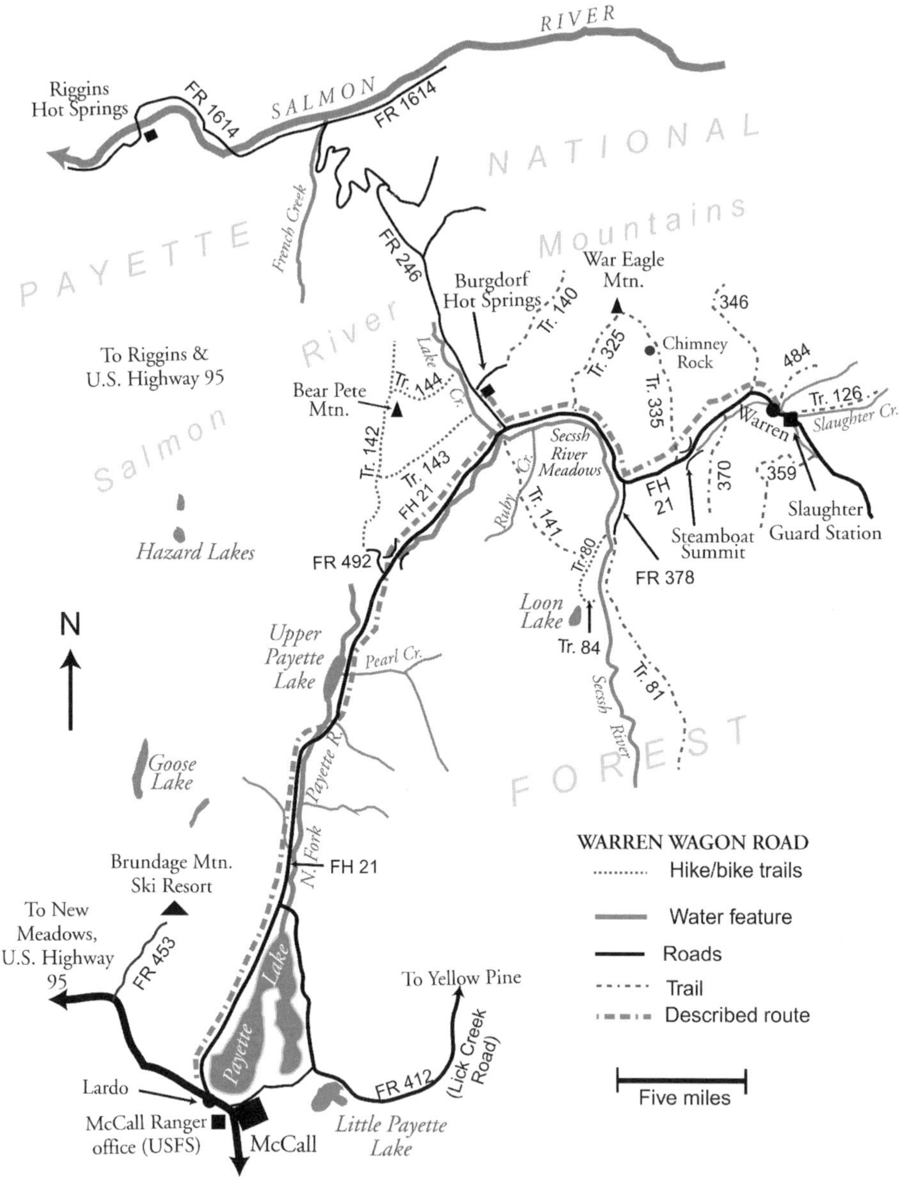

SALMON RIVER
Riggins Hot Springs
FR 1614
French Creek
PAYETTE NATIONAL FOREST
Salmon River Mountains
FR 246
Burgdorf Hot Springs
War Eagle Mtn.
Tr. 140
Tr. 325
Chimney Rock
Tr. 335
346
484
Tr. 126
Warren
Slaughter Cr.
To Riggins & U.S. Highway 95
Bear Pete Mtn.
Tr. 144
Lake Cr.
Tr. 142
Tr. 143
FH 21
Secesh River Meadows
Ruby Cr.
Tr. 141
370
359
Slaughter Guard Station
Steamboat Summit
FR 378
Hazard Lakes
FR 492
Tr. 80
Loon Lake
Tr. 84
N
Upper Payette Lake
Pearl Cr.
Secesh River
Tr. 81
Goose Lake
Payette R.
N. Fork
Brundage Mtn. Ski Resort
To New Meadows, U.S. Highway 95
FR 453
Payette Lake
To Yellow Pine
(Lick Creek Road)
FR 412
Lardo
McCall Ranger office (USFS)
McCall
Little Payette Lake
WARREN WAGON ROAD
Hike/bike trails
Water feature
Roads
Trail
Described route
Five miles

Chapter Eight

Warren Wagon Road

Midway between the north and south boundaries of Idaho, and at the southern end of Payette Lake, is located the town of McCall, a popular recreation and tourist destination. But back in 1893, before McCall could even be called a place, a freight stop a mile west of the future townsite was a bustling locus of activity. That freight stop later became known as Lardo, which has since been incorporated into McCall. What's evident there now is Lardo's Grill and Saloon, a landmark for burgers and steaks done in Western kitsch. It's also the southern terminus of the Warren Wagon Road, which leads fifty-two miles north to the gold-strike town of Warren, Idaho.

To understand this road's place in Idaho history, you must know a little about what was going on in this part of the country in the mid- and late nineteenth century. Idaho was hit with two major gold rushes in the 1860s: Silver City and Idaho City in southwest Idaho and Pierce up in the Clearwater country. From Pierce the fever of discovery swept south through Elk City and Florence in 1861, then across the Salmon River to Warren in 1862. Idaho, the territory would be created in '63; in '62 this was a remote corner of Washington Territory. Law and government were thin and far between. Surprisingly, Warren seems to have been relatively peaceful in its heyday, perhaps due to its remoteness compared to other Idaho gold strikes.

Ownership of land and rights-of-way were often sealed on a handshake, perhaps a written note; locations were blazed on a tree or marked with a stone pile. Mining rights were more of a formal matter. James Warren, who led the discovery of gold at the west end of the Salmon River Mountains, had the foresight to establish mining laws based on those used in California a decade before. This actually helped to reduce the chaos and mob rule that sometimes broke out at earlier strike sites. From the Civil War to the 1930s, this high valley in the heart of Idaho would experience cycles of explosive growth and decline.

Originally called the State Wagon Road, the Territorial Wagon Road, and just Wagon Road, the road to Warren became part of a plan to link the northern and southern parts of the state in 1889. The section from Burgdorf Junction to Warren, which also included trails that led from Grangeville and Elk City, over the Salmon River through Burgdorf and on to Warren, were also called Warren Wagon Road and Milner Trail. So cause for confusion is rife. Consider that Elk City has its own Warren Wagon Days every summer. Keep in mind that Idaho City in the Boise Basin was having its own gold rush, too, and feverous prospectors were not only coming in from the north and west, but from the south, too.

The influence of the Civil War has left a legacy of names. Because the strike at Warren occurred in 1862 when the war was rising to full pitch, refugees from the eastern U.S. brought their political loyalties and enmities with them. Two camps were established at Warren: one

Martin Potucek photo

North Beach at the mouth of the North Fork, Payette River.

called Washington (at Warren's present site) and one east called Richmond. That division proudly defined which side of the Mason-Dixon Line its residents supported. Secesh River, Secesh Summit, and Secesh Meadows indicate that secessionists held sway in the area at one time.

The actual origin of the Warren Wagon Road can not be precisely known, but as with many pioneer trails of the west, game trails likely were followed by indigenous people on hunting and migratory journeys. Using native American trails, waves of immigrants were able to improve those trails: fortune seekers of all kinds came from Europe, Asia, South America and Africa. Not just prospectors and miners, but traders and packers brought in all sorts of goods and services. Each of these parties helped to beat the trail, as did the mere passing of hundreds of heads of stock animals.

Archaeological evidence points to ancestors of the Nez Perce traveling and inhabiting this area as long as 10,000

Martin Potucek photo
Forest Highway 21 near the north end of Payette Lake.

years ago. Other evidence points to Shoshoni presence dating back 700 years. Archaeological evidence points to Nez Perce use of the meadows and hotsprings at Burgdorf, going back at least a few thousand years. Native people of the land held the hot springs of the mountains sacred; they were special places to be shared in peace.

Fred Burgdorf, who was familiar with European spas, knew these hot springs and meadows were as valuable as the gold that called from Warren. By 1870 he had established a well known stop on the trail from Elk City to Warren.

We know that pack strings of horses and mules were used as the primary supply vehicles after the mining camp at Warren was established. By 1890, the year Idaho became a state, an established wagon road had been built along the west shore of Payette Lake, and plans were afoot

Martin Potucek photo

Secesh Summit looking west. Recent fires in the area stripped the trees of foliage and made it possible to see long distance.

for pushing it farther north, up the west side of Upper Payette Lake, and over Secesh Summit. Work to make the trail accessible to wagons proceeded from both Payette Lake and Warren, working toward the middle.

Route Description

As mentioned above, the term Warren Wagon Road can mean different things. For the purposes of this chapter, we mean the road to Warren from Payette Lake.

Due to wildfires in 1994 and 2000, views from Payette Lake to Secesh Summit are excellent. This section of granite shields, peaks, and walls was scoured by Pleistocene glaciers, and the standing-dead (but regenerating) forest allows travelers to see through to places pioneers never could have. This is the western edge of the Salmon River Range that frames the mighty river drainage of the same name.

From the lake's rocky western shore the route heads north, following the North Fork of the Payette River. Many stream and river crossings in this section presented major obstacles for wagons. The grade is easy as it follows the meandering stream and increases only gradually as it leads to Upper Payette Lake where granite shields and outcroppings become more visible. From this smaller lake the grade climbs to lush and open high meadows, and then ascends to Secesh Summit.

Plunging down the north side of the summit, the route follows Summit Creek to Burgdorf Junction. It's here that Lake Creek and Summit Creek converge to form the Secesh River. Going north just a couple of miles here leads to the hot springs named after Fred Burgdorf. Following that route also leads to the main Salmon River and eventually, to the gold fields of the Clearwater country. From Burgdorf Junction, the Warren Wagon Road follows the Secesh River, which takes a more easterly direction until it goes southward into the lush Secesh Meadows. From there, the wagon road resumes an east-northeast bearing as it climbs through black pines to Steamboat Summit, the second of two major mountain passes.

Once again the road plunges down, this time from 6,694 feet elevation, following Steamboat Creek closely. Continuing east and north, dredged mine tailings mark entry into the Warren mining district. Warren is located in a narrow valley where a number of creeks join Warren and Steamboat Creeks.

Special Historical Note **

Polly Bemis: Born in Peking in 1853, the girl named Lalu Nathoy was sold by her father in 1869 to help feed the family by buying seed. Shipped to California in 1871, she was eighteen when she arrived in San Francisco. She was brought to Warren soon after that on a pack train. Polly, as she became locally known, was married to Charlie Bemis in 1894, a local merchant, after she nursed him back to health from a near fatal gunshot wound. Her friendly spirit and skill in helping others, whether they were sick or just down and out, built her a reputation of respect. The movie *A Thousand Pieces of Gold* (historical fiction) is based on her life, and a historical exhibit at St. Gertrude's Museum near Cottonwood, Idaho, is dedicated to her.

If You Want to Go

Designated now as Forest Highway 21 in the Payette National Forest of central Idaho, Warren Wagon Road runs from McCall north and east to Warren, an old mining boom town. The section of the modern road between McCall and Burgdorf Junction is surprisingly one of Idaho's best scenic highways; it's paved and with mostly wide shoulders. The remaining fifteen miles is gravel road and has only a few narrow and rocky sections. With the exception of Burgdorf Hot Springs, the Secesh Stage Stop in Secesh Meadows, and the Winter Inn in Warren, there are no services. There is no gas, but food and beverages are available at these three locations.

One option for folks going to Warren for the first time is to stop in at the District Ranger Office of the Payette National Forest in McCall; it's at the intersection of Lake and Mission, right near the center of town. You can pick up a pamphlet and accompanying CD or cassette that will guide you on an auto tour all the way to Warren.

Head west (north) out of McCall on Highway 55 (When the new highway bypass goes through, you'll come out just west of Warren Wagon Road's junction with Lake Street/Highway 55, so you'll have to jog back east or right a block or two to catch it.) This is Lardo, where Warren Wagon Road begins its route north. Follow the pavement as it winds around the western shore of Payette Lake. Watch your speed, as in the summer especially, the first few miles can be heavily congested with bikers, joggers, and kids dragging inflatables.

As you pass Sylvan Beach, the roadway comes close down to the water. To your right (east) is called the Narrows of Payette Lake; just half a mile across the water is the tip of the peninsula that gives that lake its distinctive shape. It's also the high point of the scenic loop trail the Ponderosa State Park has to offer. As you come to the north end of the lake you pass North Beach Unit of that same park; in summers here you can rent canoes to explore the winding waters of the lower North Fork of the Payette River.

Passing the end of the lake brings you along the North Fork of the Payette River. It meanders at a lazy pace for the first few miles heading upstream. A little over 1.5 miles north of the lake brings you to the former location of Fisher Station, the first roadhouse that was encountered on the route to serve travelers. It's uncertain whether another facility at Fisher Creek not quite two miles north served the same function. Traces of these buildings are now obliterated.

About three-forths mile south of the Pearl Creek turnoff is where Halfway House was located. Here another roadhouse was established for travelers on this route. For those who want to explore an intact section of the original road, you can find sections of the old trail on the west side of the river from about Pearl Creek's confluence to Upper Payette Lake.

Proceeding north another couple of miles leads to the lower end of Upper Payette Lake, which is about two miles

Martin Potucek photo

Warren Dance Hall is located in what was once the center of town.

long. Forest Highway 21 now goes up the east side of this lake and climbs more steeply than the original grade which goes left here and up the west side. If you want to detour from the existing route and follow the old route, just go left off the highway here. Forest Road 495 hugs the western shore and leads through Upper Payette Campground, about midway up the lake. The road has been blocked off past the northern end of the lake where the original road used to climb through switchbacks as the North Fork of the Payette River flows into the upper end of the lake.

Forest Highway 21 continues up and around the east side of Upper Payette Lake, and leads to Squaw Meadows, to the west. It's toward the top of these large and lush flats that the Squaw Meadows Roadhouse was located. This was a strategic location because it was just two miles below Secesh Summit. Other trails also intersected here, including a National Forest stock driveway. There may have been more than one roadhouse in close proximity at different times.

Martin Potucek photo
East end of Warren viewed from old schoolyard. The object in the foreground is a mining dredge bucket.

Another two miles up the highway brings us to Secesh Summit at 6,434 feet elevation. This is a divide between the Payette River, which drains into the Snake River and the Secesh River, which drains into the Salmon. Just north of the summit and to the west side of the roadway another roadhouse or cabin was located, but not much is known about this one; its seasonal nature can be implied by the fourteen feet of snow that piles up here each winter.

Adventure detour

If you're an avid biker/hiker, there's great access to the high trails that were probably used by pack strings almost a century ago. Just turn off left (west) before the summit onto Forest Road 492; it's a rugged dirt road that climbs to almost 7,000 ft. elevation in a little over two miles. If you drive in, park at Cloochman Saddle and then hike or bike up Trail 142 as it climbs over the ridge to Frosty Meadows and up to 8,000 ft. From here you can follow the ridge north to Burgdorf around Bear Pete Mountain (down Trail 144) or more directly down Nethker Creek ridge (Trail 143). After you hit the ridge, it's almost completely down hill. The views are spectacular, but be prepared; it's still almost ten miles the shortest way down. End detour.

As we descend the northern side of the divide we're following Summit Creek, which drains into the head of the Secesh River at Burgdorf Junction about six miles distant. Sections of the old roadway are visible from this decline.

At Burgdorf Junction, a must-stop detour is to the left here on Forest Road 246. This dirt and gravel road leads all the way to the Salmon River and on to Riggins, and for the early miners, up to Dixie, Elk City, and the Clearwater. But if you go just two miles north, you will find Burgdorf Hot Springs, a unique place for a good soak, and always some interesting folks. One of Idaho's true gems, you'll find it pretty much like it was a century ago: log-cribbed pool walls, quartz gravel pathways that glow in the dark, and no electricity. There is a phone, cabins to rent, and even a smattering of groceries. This private holding also includes a game refuge in the surrounding meadows, where seasonal elk calving can be witnessed from a distance.

Resuming our journey back at the junction, go left (east) onto Forest Highway 21 to Warren. You'll notice that the pavement ends shortly after the dumpsters, so the next 16 miles to Warren will be dirt and gravel. Watch for trucks and ATVs on the road!

The road now follows the Secesh River closely to (about 2.5 miles from Burgdorf Junction) where it crosses over to the south side of the river. Start watching for wild game as we approach the north end of Secesh Meadows, a natural haven for animals. At three miles past the junction, pass the Echo Mine or your right. Most of Secesh Meadows, which we pass through heading south, is private land; this area can be quite congested (dirt bikes, moose, etc.), so heads up! A mile farther, look for two old log structures to your right in a grassy swale; these belonged to the Fernan family who homesteaded here in the early years of the twentieth century. Their original cabin was back up the road more than a mile, but they rebuilt here after the first was destroyed. Please be aware that the cabins are on private lands and are off limits to the public. Just downriver from here and on the opposite side of the road, you'll see a sign saying: Cemetery; this is where the Fernan baby twins were buried in 1905. A short trail leads to a high spot in this shady grove.

A half mile beyond the cabin ruins, cross another bridge over the Secesh, and in another half mile you'll see Forest Road 378 going right (south). A big sign indicates Chinook Campground. This is a great Forest Service campground on the Secesh River; it's also the access to a favorite hiking/biking loop to Loon Lake. That's where the remains of a ditched military aircraft from World War II can be found. Just go out Trail 080 to Trail 084, and come back 081.

Resuming Forest Highway 21 to Warren, note that this is also where we leave the Secesh as it swings south as we head northeast into Long Gulch. We climb now a few miles to Steamboat Summit (the highest point on our trip) and the last major obstacle on our way to Warren. But this area was more than just a high pass. Just back down the road, Trail 335 heads off north past Chimney Rock and onto War Eagle Mountain, Humboldt Mine, and an entire mining district. It was also an alternate route to the main Salmon just north.

Martin Potucek photo

Warren Guard Station at east end of town. The water cannon or "monitor" displayed in front of the station used a high pressure stream of water to wash away topsoil to reveal gold deposits.

From the summit we plunge northeast following Steamboat Creek. All along this descent keep your eyes peeled for traces of the original wagon road as the newer route intertwines with the old one. About four miles from the summit we come to a bridge crossing Warren Creek; this open valley is where Steamboat, Warren, and Stratton Creeks come together. You've probably noticed the tailings piles the last couple of miles on Steamboat Creek. This was an area of huge placer operations, and these are the remains, the waste material left over.

You're in the Warren district now, and if you know where to look, signs of mining activity going back 140 years can be found. Keep in mind, if you wander the trails and sites around Warren, that anything found here must be left here. Because of ongoing archaeological study, it's best not to touch items found in or on the ground. Signs and markers on the Payette National Forest indicate most areas where active study is taking place. Because of recent looting, the area is being monitored. If you see suspicious activity while you're out and about there, you can report it to the local Forest Service guard station.

A Payette National Forest walking tour of historic Warren is available at the visitor center at the guard station at the east end of town. The Winter Inn offers burgers and cold beverages. Aside from viewing the old hotel, tavern, assay office, and dance hall, a hike up the hill to the cemetery is well worth it. This is mostly where the Euro-Americans were buried, but there are some notable exceptions. The Chinese cemetery is back the way we came, about a half mile from town by the west end of the landing strip. There's a nice little loop trail and signs pointing the way on the north side of the road.

Warren was the site of one of Idaho's big gold rushes, and a curious person could spend days here. My advice: take at least a couple of hours; park your vehicle and see Warren on foot. Not just the town, but all around there are placer and dredge tailings, ditches, dry reservoirs, bridges, and pieces of machinery. At one time there may have been a couple of thousand people burrowing and bustling about here like ants. And what's left is more than a ghost town; it's our heritage, and it can be quite instructive.

The lives of people who made this place what it was: Three-Fingered Smith, Polly Bemis, Ah Sam, to name a few, give a clue to the complexity of the community that built this place. Chinese and European cultures met and commingled here, and although things may not have always been tranquil or just (in the sense that we may now consider it), peace and order generally reigned. If you know a little about the history of gold rush towns in the west, that's surprising.

At one time, Forest Road 340 used to run east from Warren to Big Creek and south to Yellow Pine. That was washed out during the winter of 1997 and is closed at this writing. According to local authorities, it may re-open in the next few years. So if you've a mind, this drive to Warren may someday be done as a loop through some of Idaho's most fascinating gold country. From hot springs and music festivals (at Yellow Pine) to pack trails that lead to alpine lakes, this area has it all.

Much of the information was drawn from Payette National Forest Cultural Heritage Program pamphlets, which are available to the public at the forest headquarters in McCall. Many thanks are due to Larry Kingsbury, Payette National Forest Historian and Archaeologist, and his staff for context and content help.

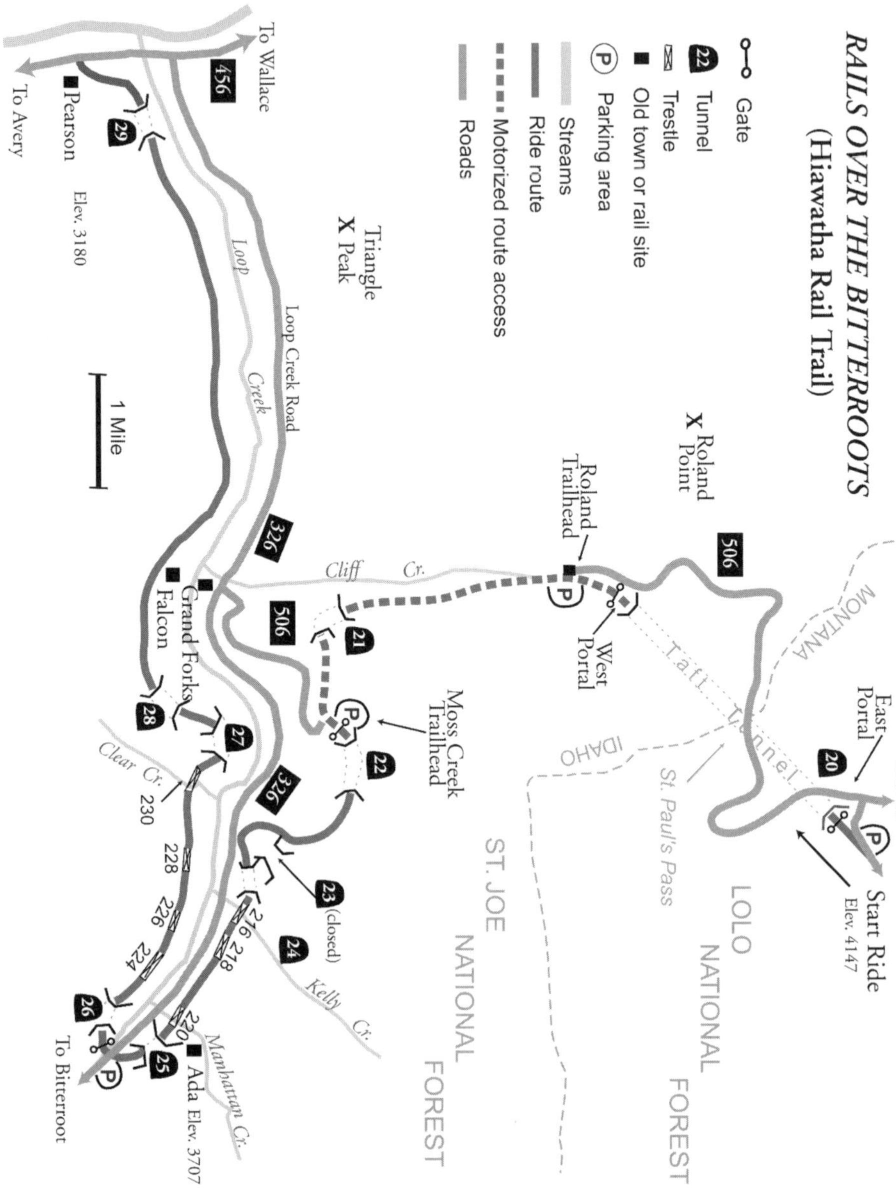
RAILS OVER THE BITTERROOTS
(Hiawatha Rail Trail)
Gate
Tunnel
Trestle
Old town or rail site
Parking area
Streams
Ride route
Motorized route access
Roads
To Wallace
To Avery
Pearson
Elev. 3180
Triangle Peak
Loop Creek
Loop Creek Road
1 Mile
Roland Point
Roland Trailhead
Cliff Cr.
Grand Forks
Falcon
West Portal
Taft Tunnel
Moss Creek Trailhead
East Portal
To I-90
Start Ride
Elev. 4147
MONTANA
IDAHO
St. Paul's Pass
LOLO NATIONAL FOREST
ST. JOE NATIONAL FOREST
Clear Cr.
Kelly Cr.
Manhattan Cr.
(closed)
Ada Elev. 3707
To Bitterroot
456
326
506
20
21
22
23
24
25
26
27
28
29
216
218
220
224
226
228
230

Chapter Nine

Railroads Through the Bitterroots

In 1878 Andrew Prichard was traveling on the Mullan Road, a military road surveyed and then built eighteen years before by Lieutenant John Mullan, of the U.S. Army. When Prichard traveled the route it was a rough and rugged track that could barely pass a wagon in places. One of the most rugged places along the entire 624 miles from Fort Benton, Montana, on the Missouri River to Walla Walla, Washington, was this section cutting through the Bitterroot Range, dividing Idaho from Montana.

Prichard found a mineral outcropping and staked the first claim in the area just west of the present town of Osborn. In 1882 he found gold to the north and staked a claim for that site, too. Although he tried to keep it to himself and just a few friends, word soon got out, and a stampede followed. By 1885 dozens of mines were producing thousands of ounces of gold and silver, and lead and zinc were also found. It became apparent soon after that mules and wagons would not do to transport the ore out and much less to bring in the heavy machinery and equipment needed to develop the mines.

Martin Potucek photo

West Portal of the Taft Tunnel, Hiawatha Rail Trail.

The first rails to reach the Coeur d'Alene basin were built in 1887. This rail line started just a half mile west of the Cataldo Mission on the Coeur d'Alene River, where steamboats coming up from Coeur d'Alene Lake could land, and extended east thirteen miles to the Bunker Hill Mine at present Kellogg. It was narrow gauge, but it allowed Bunker Hill to be the first to ship ore out of the valley on a commercial scale. In October 1887, the line was extended eleven miles east to the town of Wallace.

During the next fifteen years, while the development of the Silver Valley swung into full gear, another railroad enterprise was being hatched: a high speed line between the west coast and Chicago. This northern route would be the last of the transcontinental routes to be laid. It would allow passengers, troops, and freight to traverse the route in just two days.

In 1905 the Chicago, Milwaukee & St. Paul Railway began looking for a route for their western expansion over the Bitterroots. After almost six months, scouting over 900 miles of uncharted wilderness, the surveyors chose a route over St. Paul Pass. It crossed the boundary between Idaho and Montana, just south of where John Mullan cut his road. While Mullan's route (and I-90 that followed almost a century later) follows the St. Regis River towards its source to within a mile of Lookout Pass, the railroaders chose a route up Rainy Creek which would save them more than 500 vertical feet. That meant the rail would climb to just under 4,200 ft. in elevation, a low summit for the formidable Bitterroot Range.

Laying out a course that would punch sixteen hard rock tunnels and span seven chasms with high trestles, it was an ambitious project. Keeping the gradient to 1.7 percent on the mountain slope was necessary to insure this new main line could be kept open and running year round. There was also the millions of board feet of old growth white pine and cedar along the St. Joe River to think about. That would be an added bonus for the Milwaukee Road, as it would come to be known, as the line pushed through. The timber needed to build the trestles, tunnel supports, and buildings would take up a sizable number of those trees.

Started in 1907 and completed in 1909, the section of the Milwaukee Road between Montana and Avery, Idaho, operated until 1977. It transported troops and defense material through four wars. In the 1930s it became famous for its passenger trains with Pullman cars, fine dining, and full service luxury. Now this section has been preserved for posterity by locals and federal efforts. A hiking/biking trail has been built from East Portal on the

Montana side to Pearson, Idaho. To follow the trail, go to the last section in this chapter: If You Want to Go.

The biggest obstacle on the Milwaukee Road between the Great Plains and the Cascades was the summit of the Bitterroot Range. By digging a tunnel at St. Paul Pass (el. 4150 ft), the rail line would shave a thousand vertical feet off the Roland Summit (elevation 5,180). Approaches were prepared in 1906, and after a shaky start in 1907, the real work began in 1908. Crews dug from East Portal on the Montana side and from Roland on the Idaho side towards the middle, where they'd planned to meet. Seven hundred fifty men labored for over two years to complete the tunnel.

The St. Paul Pass Tunnel (#20 on the line) would be twenty-three feet high, sixteen feet wide, and 1.7 miles long. A steam-driven electric power plant was built at Taft on the eastern side to power the compressed air-driven steam shovels that did much of the work. Big air drills punched the holes for the charges that would blast the rock into manageable pieces. Four hundred men labored inside the tunnel when work was in full swing. It was wet, cold work with an ambient temperature just above freezing. Water pouring in from natural seams in the rock added to the difficulty. When the two crews met on March 1, 1909, they were within a fraction of an inch of being perfectly aligned.

The building of this most expensive length of line on the entire Milwaukee Road was done by immigrants from all over the globe. Almost every country in Europe was represented, as were Chinese, Japanese, and Russians. For a dollar a day, between 1907 and 1911, an international labor force built the western extension of the railroad. Disputes, old hatreds, and quarrels within and between ethnic groups resulted in occasional murder, mayhem and violence.

Martin Potucek photo
Trail head near East Portal of Taft Tunnel

Construction camp towns sprang up along the line. Grand Forks, Taft, and Adair were known for their brothels, saloons, and murders. Hospitals, hotels, and theaters also sprang up, but that didn't stop the bodies found each spring thaw during the construction heyday. Most slept in canvas tents and temporary structures, even through the winter; there was a big turnover. Surprisingly, the holocaust of the summer of 1910 diminished the conflict. Stories of everyone pulling together and daring rescues of that August abound. Also, when the railroad resorted to a bonus system for the workers, retention improved.

The relatively short period of time it took to build this stretch of the railroad was helped by the company's willingness to spend the capital and use the best, most modern tools and methods of construction. The engineers had a tight deadline, and methods of increasing efficiency were developed in the process. One technique was to build temporary wooden trestles over the gulches, lay rails and use them to bring in big machines like steam shovels, and then rebuild the permanent line with earth fill or steel trestles. It required a lot of timber, so sawmills were built, and another level of industry was added to the process.

The trestles over Kelly and Clear Creeks carried their

rails more than 200 feet above ground; this presented some special problems for the engineers. The engineers decided they would build with steel from the start. A 150-ton rolling crane, called the Traveler, was delivered, unassembled, to the site. It stood more than sixty feet high, and stretched more than 120 feet in length, counter-balanced with more than thirty tons of rails. Developed by Milwaukee engineers specifically for this job, it took nine days to put it together and get it working. The beauty of the machine was that it took a crew of only a couple dozen men just one month to erect the Kelly Creek Trestle, the highest and longest of the entire project.

A method used to fill in temporary wooden trestles with earth and rock was borrowed from the gold fields. Two large water cannons, called Monitors or Giants, were built on the Idaho side to sluice the debris loosened by the spouts. A flume fed into each of the four-inch diameter jets through a long, well-anchored twelve-inch pipe. The resulting pressure was enough to unleash a man-made, controllable (most of the time) avalanche of mud. By the end of the project in 1911, twenty-two trestles had been earth-filled between St. Regis and Avery, although most were filled with dump cars from the trestles themselves.

In 1909 the Milwaukee Road built a two-story depot in Roland, at the western end of the St. Paul Pass Tunnel. Up until that point, it had been a canvas and tarpaper camp for the tunnel workers. Electricity came later that year after the tunnel bore was completed. A hand-operated turntable called "The Beast of the Bitterroots" could rotate a twenty-ton locomotive 180 degrees. Most likely, the image of the "beast" came from those who had to apply their shoulders to the push bars. Roland was abandoned in the early 1960s when the depot was demolished and the bunkhouses were moved to East Portal. Only the footings for the depot and powder magazine remain.

On August 20 and 21, 1910, a big wind blew up a number of smaller, independent fires into a firestorm. While it was happening all over the Idaho Panhandle, this was one place where the fuel was thick and ready to burn. It was especially vulnerable because of the concentrated populations building the line, surrounded closely by abundant fuel. More than 100 people were rescued on August 20 when a brave engineer loaded terrified workers and their families onto a flatcar at Falcon and raced the fire to Tunnel 27 and safety. J. Mackedon, the engineer, describes throwing the locomotive into full throttle and everyone laying out flat to protect themselves as they penetrated a wall of flame.

The railroad survived the conflagration of 1910; amazingly only one death in the area was reported. Danger from unchecked runoff the following spring would add to the work of repairing the damage. It would take decades for the forest to regenerate around the line, but what was next to come was a minor modern miracle.

In 1912, the Milwaukee Road's directors started a project that would electrify the rail line from Harlowton, Montana, to Avery, Idaho. In 1917 this section began operation. The success of this initial project encouraged the railroad to try it between Othello and Tacoma, Washington. When that section was completed, the Milwaukee had the longest stretches of electrified mainline in the world, totaling 647 miles.

The electric locomotives made a lot of sense. Electricity was cheaper to produce than the oil-fired steam used then in most locomotives. It was also cleaner and safer, especially in the long tunnels in the Rockies and Cascades. Water for hydro-power was abundant in the region and

Martin Potucek photo
Rail Trail trestle with overhead catenaries still in place. Catenaries support the wire that feeds power to electric locomotives.

was close by. Another advantage of electric over steam power was only apparent in the winter; while boilers were robbed of much of their heat (and thus—power) in the extreme cold of winter, electric motors ran at the same efficiency no matter what the ambient temperature. And it didn't hurt that some board members owned interests in Montana copper mines and Idaho dams that generated the power.

A catenary system fed power from a substation to the locomotives via live electric wires. These wires followed the rails overhead (suspended from wooden arms) to the electric motors on the engines, much like electric trolley cars in cities today. It took special skills and a lot of learning on the way, for this was new technology of the time. Occasional pieces would go out to the national and international press about the marvels of this new application of electricity. Maintenance workers needed special tools and methods; many times those were created in the process, like the special Dodge Power Wagon trucks that were used in the 1950s. They were rolling maintenance derricks that would allow workers to keep the power flowing smoothly.

Winters near the summit usually closed the local roads, so in the '20s, '30s, and '40s, local residents either used borrowed "motor cars" that ran on the rails, or they developed their own solutions to winter travel. One family at East Portal built a pusher propeller-driven vehicle that ran on skis, an early precursor of today's snowmobiles. There was even a period from the late '30s to 1941 (the start of World War II) when the railroad got permission from the Forest Service to cut a ski run from Roland down to Loop Creek and operate a "ski basin." Scheduled ski trains brought adventurous skiers from Spokane, Missoula, and St. Maries to spend the day at the ski bowl and then whisk them back the same evening. Huge rotary snow plows kept the line open, even when fifteen feet of snow piled up around them.

From 1937 until the 1960s the Milwaukee Road operated luxury passenger trains from Chicago to Seattle. With Pullman sleeper cars, full porter service, and fine dining, this mode of travel became famous across the country. In 1947, the streamlined Olympian Hiawatha was introduced; fast and smooth, these trains pampered their passengers. In 1952, Super Dome cars replaced the older lounge cars, allowing passengers to view the sights without craning out the windows. Even more impressive was the trailing car on these trains: the Sky Top Lounge, a rounded, futuristic-looking cabin with a domed glass ceiling and cocktail service.

The period of the Olympian Hiawatha was perhaps the pinnacle of the Milwaukee Road's history. The 1950s brought on the building of an interstate highway system with more comfortable automobiles to travel those roads. The opening of the Panama Canal in 1914 had an effect on the freight tonnage the line would carry. The advent of jet travel would spell the end for its passenger service in

1961. Having survived bankruptcies and reorganizations in 1925, 1927, 1935, and 1945, the Milwaukee ended service in 1979, with the final remnants sold off in 1985.

In the mid-nineties work began between the Forest Service and private individuals to create a recreational trail, open to the public, on the part of the line that traversed the Bitterroot Range. By the summer of 1997, the spectacular stretch between St. Paul Pass on the Montana-Idaho border and Pearson, Idaho, was opened. In only thirteen miles, eleven hard rock tunnels and nine steel trestles are preserved and passable. Surface grading, signs, and safety railings were added, with the help of hundreds of local, private, and Forest Service workers.

The crown jewel of the mostly non-motorized Idaho section was completed two years later; this was the Taft Tunnel, a 1.7 mile-long hard rock bore through the crest of the Bitterroots. A fee is charged for the Idaho section from East Portal to Pearson, and is administered by the Taft Tunnel Preservation Society. This section is also part of a longer forty-six-mile recreational route that follows the old Milwaukee from St. Regis, Montana, to Avery, Idaho. It has received attention nationally, through *National Geographic*, *Outside*, and *Sunset* magazines, and was made a National Heritage Trail in 1999.

If You Want to Go

The Hiawatha Rail Trail is located on the Idaho-Montana border, south of Interstate 90 in the Bitterroot Range. You can bring your own bikes, or rent and get info at the Lookout Pass Ski Area in summer. You need a light, helmet, probably a sweater, if you go through the Taft Tunnel (temperature thirty-three degrees F.); it's also pitch black. The trail drops only 300 feet in more than seven miles, so the grade is very gentle. It's on Lolo and

Idaho Panhandle National Forest land. A shuttle service is also available; for schedules and rates, just ask at Lookout Pass.

From Coeur d'Alene, take I-90 east about sixty miles to Exit O, Lookout Pass Ski Area, if you need to rent a bike, light, or to arrange for a shuttle return ride; this is the headquarters of the trail concession. If you're ready to roll, go another five miles east into Montana and take Exit 5. From here, go left at a Tee, follow signs to Route of the Hiawatha. Go another eighth of a mile and take a right onto Forest Road 506 (Rainy Creek Road). Follow another two miles to East Portal trailhead. As you come in sight of the trailhead, bear left at fork; there's parking here. Going to the right will take you up over the Roland Summit and to the west portal of the Taft Tunnel (for those who don't want to travel the long tunnel, but still want access to the rail trail). Autos can also climb over the Roland Summit and bypass the long tunnel; a dirt and gravel driving route will also lead you out to Avery and the St. Joe River.

THE AUTHOR

Penny Schwyn

Martin Potucek has lived in Idaho since 1972. He has done everything from build homes in Bonner County to teach writing at the University of Idaho. He has skied, climbed and biked over much of the state. Boise and McCall have been his most recent haunts. He and his family recently moved to Spokane, Washington, which, the way they play it, is really part of north Idaho.

Martin has written two mountain biking guides for Falcon Press, one for Boise and one for the Spokane-Coeur d' Alene areas.

BIBLIOGRAPHY

A Short Story of Idaho, Idaho State Historical Society, Boise, Idaho, 1974

Astoria, Washington Irving, J. B. Millar, NY, 1885

The Bear River Massacre, Newell Hart, Cache Valley Newsletter Publishing, Preston, ID, 1982

Bird Woman (Sacajewea), J. W. Schultz, Houghton Mifflin, NY, 1918

Blazing a Wagon Trail to Oregon, L. W. Coffman, Echo Books, Enterprise, OR, 1993.

Chief Joseph Country, Bill Gulick, Caxton Printers, Caldwell, ID, 1981 (good maps).

Children of Grace, The Nez Perce War of 1877, B. Hampton, Holt, 1993

Conquest of the Coeur d' Alenes, Spokanes and Palouses, B. F. Manring, Ye Galeon, 1975

Early History of Idaho, W. J. McConnell, Caxton Printers, Caldwell, Idaho, 1913

The Expedition of Lewis and Clark, M. Lewis, University Microfilms, 1966

The Flight of the Nez Perce, A History of the Nez Perce War, Mark Brown, Putnam, 1967

Following the Nez Perce Trail, Cheryl Wilfong, Oregon State University Press, 1990

General George Wright, Guardian of the Pacific Coast, Carl Schlicke, University of Oklahoma Press, 1988

Hear Me, My Chiefs!, L. V. McWhorter, Caxton Printers, Caldwell, Idaho, 1952

Idaho Lore, ed. Vardis Fisher, Caxton Printers, 1939, Federal Writers Project (WPA)

Idaho Place Names, Lalia Boone, U of I Press, Moscow, Idaho, 1988

I Will Fight No More Forever – Chief Joseph and the Nez Perce War, Merrill D. Beal, U of Washington Press, 1963

I Will Tell My War Story, Scott M. Thompson, U of Washington Press with ISHS, 2000

Idaho – An Illustrated History, Merle Wells, ISHS, 1976

In Mountain Shadows, A History of Idaho, Carlos Schwantes, U of Nebraska Press, 1991.

In the Footsteps of Lewis and Clark , G.S. Snyder, *National Geographic*, 1970

The Journals of Lewis and Clark, ed. Bernard DeVoto, Houghton Mifflin, 1953

Ka-mi-akin, the Last Hero of the Yakimas, A. J. Splawn, Kilham Printing, Portland, Oregon, 1917.

Lewis and Clark in Idaho, J. Peebles, Idaho Historical Society, Boise, Idaho, 1966

The Lewis and Clark Trail, A. Satterfield, Stackpole Press, Harrisburg, Pennsylvania, 1978

The Lolo Trail, A History and Guide to the Trail of Lewis and Clark, Ralph S. Spence, Historic Montana Publishing, Missoula, 2001

Nez Perce Country, National Park Service, U.S. Dept. of Interior, 1983

Nez Perce Indian War and Original Stories, N. B. Adkison, Idaho County Free Press, Grangeville, Idaho, 1966

Nez Perce Summer, 1877, J. A. Greene, Montana Historical Society Press, Helena, 2000

Noon Ne-Me-Poo, Allen Slickpoo, Sr., Nez Perce Tribe of Idaho, 1973.

The Original Northwester, David Thompson and the Native Tribes of North America, Rowland Bond, Spokane House Enterprises, 1970

The Saga of Lewis and Clark into the Uncharted West, Thomas and Jeremy Schmidt, DK Publishing, New York, New York, 1999

The Shoshoni Frontier and the Bear River Massacre, B. D. Madsen, U of Utah, 1985

The Bloody Deed, The Magruder Incident, Ladd Hamilton, WSU Press, 1994

Tsceminicum, Land of Coyote, Tom Beall, R. D. Leeper, State Dept. of Education, Idaho, 1971

Warbonnets and Epaulets, Jerome Peltier, Payette Radio Ltd., Montreal, 1965

Yellow Wolf: His Own Story, L. V. McWhorter, Caxton Printers, Caldwell, Idaho, 1948

Other Books From CAXTON PRESS

Gem Minerals of Idaho

ISBN 0-87004-228-9 Paper $9.95

6x9 129 pages photographs $9.95

Southern Idaho Ghost Towns

ISBN 0-87004-229-7

6x9 135 pages 14 maps paper $12.95

River Tales of Idaho

ISBN 0-87004-378-1

6x9 344 pages illustrated maps paper $17.95

Do Them No Harm! Lewis & Clark among the Nez Perce

ISBN 0-87004-427-3

6x9 350 pages illustrations, paper $16.95

Shoshoni Pony

ISBN 0-87004-431-1

11x8 32 pages color illustration Hardcover $15.95

Dreamers On the Trail of the Nez Perce

ISBN 0-87004-393-5

6x9 450 pages, illustrated Hardcover $24.95

For a free Caxton catalog write to:

CAXTON PRESS
312 Main Street
Caldwell, ID 83605-3299

or

Visit our Internet Website:

www.caxtonpress.com

Caxton Press is a division of The CAXTON PRINTERS, Ltd.

WC